Historical Association Studies

The Making of Modern South Africa

Historical Association Studies

General Editors: Muriel Chamberlain and H. T. Dickinson

China in the Twentieth Century
Paul Bailey

The Agricultural Revolution
John Beckett

Class, Party and the Political System
in Britain 1867–1914
John Belchem

Ireland 1828–1923: From Ascendancy
to Democracy
D. George Boyce

The Ancien Régime
Peter Campbell

Decolonization: The Fall of the
European Empires
M.E. Chamberlain

Gandhi
Anthony Copley

The Counter-Reformation
N.S. Davidson

British Radicalism and the French
Revolution
H.T. Dickinson

From Luddism to the First Reform
Bill: Reform in England 1810–1832
J.R. Dinwiddy

Radicalism in the English Revolution
1640–1660
F.D. Dow

British Politics Since 1945: The Rise
and Fall of Consensus
David Dutton

The Spanish Civil War
Sheelagh M. Ellwood

The French Revolution
Alan Forrest

Revolution and Counter-Revolution in
France 1815–1852
William Fortescue

The New Monarchy: England
1471–1534
Anthony Goodman

The French Reformation
Mark Greengrass

Britain and European Cooperation
Since 1945
Sean Greenwood

Politics in the Reign of Charles II
K.H.D. Haley

Occupied France: Collaboration and
Resistance 1940–1944
H.R. Kedward

The Vikings in Britain
Henry Loyn

Secrecy in Britain
Clive Ponting

Women in an Industrializing Society:
England 1750–1880
Jane Rendall

Appeasement
Keith Robbins

Franklin D. Roosevelt
Michael Simpson

Britain's Decline: Problems and
Perspectives
Alan Sked

The Cold War 1945–1965
Joseph Smith

Britain in the 1930s
Andrew Thorpe

The Normans in Britain
David Walker

Bismarck
Bruce Waller

The Russian Revolution 1917–1921
Beryl Williams

The Making of Modern South Africa
Nigel Worden

Lloyd George
Chris Wrigley

The Historical Association, founded in 1906, brings together people who share an
interest in, and love for, the past. It aims to further the study and teaching of history at
all levels: teacher and student, amateur and professional. This is one of over 100
publications available at preferential rates to members. Membership also includes
journals at generous discounts and gives access to courses, conferences, tours and
regional and local activities. Full details are available from The Secretary, The
Historical Association, 59a Kennington Park Road, London SE11 4JH, telephone:
0171–735 3901.

The Making of Modern South Africa: Conquest, Segregation and Apartheid

Second Edition

Nigel Worden

BLACKWELL
Oxford UK & Cambridge USA

Copyright © Nigel Worden, 1994, 1995

The right of Nigel Worden to be identified as author of this work has been asserted in accordance with the Copyright, Designs and Patents Act 1988.

First published 1994

Second edition 1995

Blackwell Publishers Ltd
108 Cowley Road
Oxford OX4 1JF
UK

Blackwell Publishers Inc.
238 Main Street
Cambridge, Massachusetts 02142
USA

British Library Cataloguing in Publication Data
A CIP catalogue record for this book is available from the British Library.

Library of Congress Cataloging-in-Publication Data has been applied for.

ISBN 0–631–19882–2

Typeset in Erhardt 10/12pt
by Photoprint, Torquay, Devon
Printed and bound in Great Britain by Hartnolls Limited, Bodmin, Cornwall

This book is printed on acid-free paper

For my parents, Vena and John

Contents

List of Maps   viii

Outline Chronology   ix

Acknowledgements   xv

List of Acronyms   xvi

1 Introduction: The Changing History of South Africa   1
2 The Conquest of the Land   5
3 Changes in Town and Countryside   34
4 White Supremacy, Segregation and Apartheid   65
5 The Heyday of Apartheid   95
6 Apartheid in Decline   121

Bibliography   147

Index   163

Maps

1   African societies in the nineteenth century   13

2   The Union of South Africa, 1910   31

3   'Native Reserves', 1913 and 1936   49

4   The Bantustans (Homelands)   110

5   South African Provinces   142

Outline Chronology

c.1000 BC	'Pastoralist revolution': Khoikhoi herders move into South Africa
AD 300–1000	Bantu-speaking farmers move into South Africa
1652	Dutch East India Company establishes settlement at Cape Town
1650s–1780s	Colonial expansion into northern and eastern Cape and conquest of Khoikhoi
1658	First slaves imported to Cape
1760s	Slaves and Khoi obliged to carry passes
1799–1803	Khoikhoi rebellion in eastern Cape
1806	British establish permanent control over Cape Colony
1812	Indenture of Khoi children on settler farms
1820s	Expansion of Zulu kingdom ('Mfecane')
1828	Ordinance 49 imposes pass controls on African workers in Cape Colony; Ordinance 50 ends Khoi indenture
1834	Slave emancipation
1836	Settlers leave eastern Cape ('Great Trek')
1838	Trekkers defeat Zulu and establish Republic of Natalia (Natal)
1843	British annexation of Natal
1846	Shepstone introduces segregated administration for Africans in Natal
1852	Sand River Convention: British recognize Boer independence in region north of the Vaal River (Transvaal)
1854	Bloemfontein Convention: British recognize Orange

	Free State; Cape Colony obtains Representative Government
1856–7	Xhosa cattle-killing
1860	Introduction of Indian indentured labourers to Natal (ended 1911)
1866	Cape annexes British Kaffraria
1867	Discovery of diamonds at Vaal-Hartz river (Kimberley)
1871	British annex diamond fields (Griqualand West)
1872	Cape obtains Responsible Government
1875	'Black Flag' revolt at Kimberley
1877	British annex Transvaal
1875	Foundation of Genootskap van Regte Afrikaaners (Paarl)
1878	British defeat Thlaping (Tswana) rebellion in Griqualand West
1879	British invasion of Zululand; British defeat Pedi
1879–85	Transkei annexed to Cape Colony
1880	Griqualand West annexed to Cape Colony; Cape war with Sotho; Foundation of Afrikaner Bond (Cape)
1881	Transvaal rebellion forces British withdrawal
1882	Foundation of Imbumba ya Manyama (eastern Cape)
1884–5	British annex southern Bechuanaland
1886	Gold discovered on Witwatersrand (Johannesburg)
1887	British annex Zululand
1893	Natal obtains Responsible Government
1894	Glen Grey Act establishes separate land and tax system for Africans (eastern Cape)
1895	Southern Bechuanaland annexed to Cape Colony; Transvaal government asserts control over Swaziland; Jameson Raid from Cape fails to topple Transvaal government
1896–7	Rinderpest epidemic
1896	Thlaping revolt (Langeberg) defeated by British
1897	Zululand annexed to Natal
1899–1902	South African ('Boer') War: British conquest of Transvaal and Orange Free State
1902–5	'Reconstruction' of Transvaal and Free State under Milner
1902	Foundation of African People's Organisation (APO)

	in Cape Town; Treaty of Vereeniging ends South African War
1903–5	South African Native Affairs Commission recommends blueprint for segregation
1904–7	Chinese indentured labourers used on gold mines
1907	Election victory of Het Volk (Transvaal) and Orangia Unie (Orange River Colony)
1906–8	Bambatha (Zulu) rebellion defeated
1910	Union of South Africa
1911	Mines and Works Act imposes colour bar in mines
1912	Foundation of SANNC (later ANC)
1913	Natives Land Act segregates land ownership and restricts African land ownership to the 'native reserves'; Indian general strike in Natal led by Gandhi
1913–14	White strikes on Rand
1914	South Africa enters First World War; Afrikaner rebellion
1915	South African invasion of German South West Africa
1918	Status Quo Act modifies job colour bar on mines; African municipal workers strike in Johannesburg; Foundation of Afrikaner Broederbond
1919	Foundation of ICU
1920	Native Affairs Act establishes separate administrative structures for Africans; African mineworkers strike
1921	Massacre of 'Israelites' at Bulhoek
1922	Rand Revolt
1923	Natives (Urban Areas) Act provides for urban segregation and African influx control; Industrial Conciliation Act excludes migrant workers from trade union representation
1924	Coalition of Labour and National Party win election: 'Pact' government under Hertzog; Afrikaans given official recognition
1926	Mines and Works Amendment Act extends employment colour bar
1927	Native Administration Act 'retribalizes' African government and law
1930–3	Great Depression
1932	Native Service Contract Act restricts black labour

	tenants on white-owned farms; South Africa abandons gold standard
1934	South African Party (under Smuts) and National Party (under Hertzog) form coalition 'Fusion' government; Slums Act gives local municipalities right to move inhabitants of low-grade housing
1935	Formation of All African Convention (AAC)
1936	Native Trust and Land Act consolidates reserves; Representation of Natives Act removes Africans from Cape common franchise
1937	Marketing Act gives state subsidies to white farmers; Native Laws Amendment Act intensifies urban pass laws
1938	*Eeuwfees* centenary celebration of Great Trek mobilizes Afrikaner nationalism
1940–5	Rent and transport boycotts and squatter resistance on Rand
1941	Formation of Council for Non-European Trade Unions
1943	Non-European Unity Movement produces 'Ten Point Programme'; Foundation of ANC Youth League
1946	African Mineworkers strike
1946–7	Natal Indian Congress resists 'Ghetto' Act restricting Indian property ownership
1946	Sauer report recommends intensification of segregation
1948	'Herstigte' Nationalist Party forms government
1949	ANC Youth League produces 'Programme of Action'; African and Indian conflict in Durban
1950	Population Registration Act; Immorality Act; Group Areas Act; Suppression of Communism Act
1951	Bantu Authorities Act
1952	Abolition of Passes and Coordination of Documents Act extends pass laws; ANC launches 'Defiance Campaign'
1953	Separate Amenities Act; Bantu Education Act; Criminal Law Amendment Act
1953–4	Resistance to destruction of Sophiatown
1955	Native (Urban Areas) Amendment Act extends urban

	influx control; National Congress of the People adopts 'Freedom Charter'
1956	Coloureds removed from Cape common franchise; Mass demonstration of women against pass laws
1956–61	Treason trial
1956–7	Rural revolts in Transvaal and Free State
1957	Alexandra bus boycotts
1959	Foundation of Pan African Congress (PAC); Promotion of Bantu Self-Governing Act sets up ethnic 'homelands'; Cato Manor (Durban) beerhall protests
1960	Sharpeville shootings and State of Emergency; Banning of ANC, Communist Party and PAC; Pondoland revolt
1961	Umkhonto we Sizwe guerrilla movement founded; Poqo revolt; South Africa leaves Commonwealth and becomes a Republic
1963	General Laws Amendment Act permits detention without trial
1964	Rivonia trials sentence ANC leaders to life imprisonment; Black Labour Act tightens influx control
1969	Foundation of South African Students' Organisation (SASO) under Biko
1971	Establishment of Black People's Convention (BPC)
1973–5	Widespread African strikes in Natal and eastern Cape
1975	Foundation of Inkatha under Buthelezi
1976	Revolt in Soweto and other townships
1977	Detention and murder of Biko; banning of Black Consciousness organizations
1976–81	Nominal independence of homelands: Transkei (1976), Bophuthatswana (1977), Venda (1979), Ciskei (1981)
1978	P.W. Botha introduces 'total strategy' policy; Foundation of Azanian People's Organisation (AZAPO)
1979	Carlton Conference meeting of government and business leaders; Riekert Commission recommends easing of job colour bar; Wiehahn Commission recommends recognition of African trade unions
1982	Formation of Conservative Party under Treurnicht
1982	Black Local Authorities Act extends Community Council powers in townships
1983	Foundation of National Forum (NF) and United

	Democratic Front (UDF)
1984	Elections under new tricameral constitution widely boycotted by Indian and Coloured voters
1984–6	Widespread resistance; State of Emergency and troops moved into townships
1985	Foundation of Congress of South African Trade Unions (COSATU); International bank loans called in and sanctions intensified; Uitenhage shootings; National Education Crisis Committee (NECC) calls for 'People's Education'; Conflict in Inanda (Natal)
1986	Repeal of pass laws; Commonwealth delegation visit aborted by South African raids on neighbouring countries
1986–9	Widespread conflict between Inkatha and UDF in Natal
1988	KwaNdebele resistance to 'independence'
1989	Botha replaced by F.W. de Klerk; Mass Democratic Movement (MDM) launches civil disobedience campaign
1990	De Klerk unbans ANC, PAC and Communist Party; Nelson Mandela released from jail; Namibia obtains independence
1991	Repeal of Group Areas, Land, and Population Registration Acts; Convention for a Democratic South Africa (CODESA) formed to negotiate democratic constitution; Government backing of Inkatha vigilantes against ANC
1992	White referendum supports CODESA negotiations but they break down and Inkatha–ANC conflict intensifies
1993	Negotiations resumed at Kempton Park to form interim constitution
1994	Election by universal franchise elects Government of National Unity with ANC majority; Mandela inaugurated as State President

Acknowledgements

As the references and bibliography show, I am indebted to a large number of historians of South Africa for the content of this book. In the process of summarizing and selecting I hope that I have not offended any of them too much. In addition I am particularly grateful to Russell Martin, Christopher Saunders, Iain Smith and James Patrick who saved me from a number of factual and stylistic infelicities. None of them, needless to say, are responsible for the misjudgements which may remain.

Acronyms

ANC	African National Congress
APO	African People's Organisation
AWB	Afrikaner Weerstand Beweging
AAC	All African Convention
APLA	Azanian People's Liberation Army
AZAPO	Azanian People's Organisation
BPC	Black People's Convention
COSATU	Congress of South African Trade Unions
CODESA	Convention for a Democratic South Africa
COSAG	Concerned South Africans Group
CP	Conservative Party
DP	Democratic Party
ECC	End Conscription Campaign
FAK	Federasie van Afrikaanse Kultuurverenigings
FF	Freedom Front
ICU	Industrial and Commercial Workers' Union
IFP	Inkatha Freedom Party
MDM	Mass Democratic Movement
NF	National Forum
NP	National Party
NEUM	Non European Unity Movement
PAC	Pan Africanist Congress
SACP	South African Communist Party
SANAC	South African Native Affairs Commission
SASO	South African Students Organisation
SWAPO	South West African People's Organisation
UDF	United Democratic Front
UWUSA	United Workers Union of South Africa
VOC	Dutch East India Company

1

Introduction: The Changing History of South Africa

Over the past two decades South Africa has been much in the public eye. Events such as the Soweto uprising of 1976, the virtual civil war of the mid-1980s and the release in 1990 of Nelson Mandela, the 'world's most famous political prisoner', brought wide international attention and condemnation to a country whose policies of legislated racial discrimination made it an anomaly in the post-colonial world. The painful transition of South Africa towards democracy was watched with international concern and interest.

Over the same period, study of South Africa's past has mushroomed. Many new academic works appeared from the mid-1970s and university courses on South African history were offered widely in Europe, the United States and Africa. Not only did the volume of scholarship increase: its general findings significantly transformed our understanding of the making of modern South Africa in a process which 'in historiographical terms represents a revolution' (Smith 1988).

This book attempts to introduce readers to some of this new historical scholarship. It may be read as a self-contained work although it is not a complete general history of South Africa, and the reader may choose to supplement it with one of the several good recent overviews on the market (see general surveys, p. 142). Although it ranges from the pre-colonial period to the present, its central focus is on the years between the 1910s and the 1960s, when the system of segregation and apartheid was developed.

The themes I have chosen reflect the focus of writing on South African history at the beginning of the 1990s. To understand how

1

these emerged we need to say something briefly about the prevailing views that preceded it.

The earliest histories of South Africa were concerned with its white inhabitants. They varied greatly in their perspective: Afrikaner nationalist writers tended to laud the achievements of the trekkers and their descendents, whilst English-speaking historians placed emphasis on the role of the British government and settlers. As in Europe, many histories written in the early twentieth century emphasized political events and the 'making of the nation state'. Such approaches pervaded general texts well into the 1970s (for instance Muller 1975) and continued to dominate South African school syllabi into the 1990s.

But by the middle of the century the inadequacy of such an approach was apparent. Clearly the key issue in South Africa was race and the causes of systematic segregation. Historians of liberal sympathies began to explore these issues, emphasizing the economic and social background to segregation and apartheid. Despite diversity, most of these writers viewed South Africa as a 'dual economy' with two distinct societies: a white urban and capitalist agrarian system on the one hand and a rural impoverished and stagnating African sector on the other. Apartheid was explained by the unhappy history of a virulent racism, primarily of Afrikaners, which was born on the frontier of the early Cape colony and transported inland by the Great Trek to resurface in the catastrophic National Party victory of 1948. Such arguments were the mainstay of the authoritative *Oxford History of South Africa* published in the late 1960s and early 1970s (Wilson and Thompson 1971).

The *Oxford History* also foreshadowed changes in historical approach of a more fundamental nature. It was influenced by the emergence of African history as a sub-discipline in its own right in the late 1960s and 1970s. In response to the independence of Africa from colonialism a body of scholarship now focused on the internal operation of African societies, rather than seeing them as adjuncts to colonial policies. It was no longer possible to view South African history as the story of British and Afrikaner settlers and their conflicts.

But the South African 'historiographical revolution' went further than this. Indeed the *Oxford History* was criticized soon after its publication by a new group of young historians who were influenced by a neo-Marxist, or revisionist, paradigm. They explained apartheid not by the irrational racism of a pre-industrial colonial frontier, but as the direct product of South Africa's unique process of industrialization. Segregation, so argued the revisionists, was specifically developed to nurture early industry, particularly mining, and capitalist agriculture. Contrary to the 'dual economy' notion of the liberals, revisionists saw the poverty and deprivation of many Africans as an integral part of the South African industrial system. Cheap labour was the basis of this economy, and it explained much of the growth and dynamics of modern South Africa. In this argument segregation and apartheid resulted from class domination by capitalists rather than broad race domination by whites.

These approaches transformed our understanding of the South African past. The focus now lay on early industrialization on the Rand after the 1880s rather than on the societies of the pre-industrial trekker republics and British colonies in the early nineteenth century. The nature of specific class formations in differing periods and regions came to be identified. Not all whites or all Africans underwent the same experiences. For instance, Afrikaner nationalism had to be consciously created in the 1930s as a means of bringing together diverse class interests. And a vibrant African peasant sector was identified in the late nineteenth century, initially responding to new market opportunities but then being destroyed by the competing needs of white farmers and urban employers for labour.

In the course of the past twenty years some of the dogmatism of the early revisionist writers has been tempered. In particular, following trends in historical writing elsewhere, the crude structuralism of Marxist argument has given way to a more nuanced version, in which individual and community experiences have been given prime place and the diversity of response is now recognized. But the central theme of the link between racial domination and capitalist growth in the early twentieth century remains unchallenged.

Undoubtedly the hegemony of this approach will give way to new paradigms in the future. Already there are new themes and areas of emphasis in historical work, such as the causes of the dislocation of African societies in the 1820s (Cobbing 1988; Eldredge 1992) or the structures of power and labour control following slave emancipation in the mid-nineteenth-century Cape (Worden and Crais 1994). The importance of gender is only beginning to be acknowledged as a category of historical analysis alongside race and class (Walker 1990). Changing interpretation and emphasis is a necessary sign of thriving scholarship. But the impact of the revisionist 'revolution' continues to be decisive in framing new questions and hence new answers.

The emphasis of this book is on the latest work. As a result many traditional themes are given less attention. The dynamics of white politics, for instance, are little considered and events such as the 'Great Trek' or the 'Boer War' are included as part of broader developments. In their place are the benchmarks of the new work which were virtually ignored in earlier writings, such as the dynamics behind colonial conquest in the late nineteenth century, the mineral revolution of the 1880s, white worker militancy in the late 1910s and black rural protest in the 1920s. The roots and emergence of segregation is a prime theme, setting the context for modern apartheid. Although there is a broad chronological progression throughout the book, chapters 3 and 4 emphasize differing themes which span across a wide period. Frequent references are provided to the writings on which this material is based for those who wish to read further. Although there are still large gaps in our understanding of aspects of the South African past, the key processes are reflected in these pages.

SUGGESTIONS FOR FURTHER READING

Smith, I. 1988: 'The revolution in South African historiography'. *History Today*, 38, February, 8–10.
Smith, K. 1988: *The changing past: trends in South African historical writing.* Johannesburg: Southern Books.
Saunders, S. 1988: *The making of the South African past: major historians on race and class.* Cape Town: David Philip.

2

The Conquest of the Land

South Africa emerged as a state less than a century ago. The diverse polities of the region were brought together for the first time by the Act of Union of 1910. This was only made possible by the encroachment of colonial power over the region during the eighteenth and nineteenth centuries.

Contrary to the traditions of settler and colonial historiography, however, the conquest of South Africa by people of European origin was by no means a steady or an inevitable one but was marked by setbacks, uneven population movements and uncertain goals. As late as the 1870s the sub-continent was divided into a large number of polities, chiefdoms, colonies and settlements of widely differing size, power and racial composition, without political unity or cohesion. Yet within fifty years a unified and distinctively capitalist nation had come into being which was an integral part of the British Empire, was ruled by whites and had firmly entrenched colonial and settler interests. The conquest of the land thus provides the essential background to the history of modern South Africa.

Pre-colonial developments

One of the many myths perpetuated until quite recently in South African history held that colonists moved into an 'empty land', or at least only began to settle in the interior of the region at about the same time as indigenous pastoralists and cultivators were moving into it from the north. Clearly this view served to legitimize the claims of whites to

5

land occupation in a later period. However, it is only in the past couple of decades that archaeological and historical work has focused on the real situation before the arrival of white colonists in the region.

There were several major processes of population movement and settlement in South Africa before colonial penetration began in the late seventeenth century. From at least the Late Stone Age the region was widely inhabited by hunting and gathering San people. Surviving San groups now only live in the arid regions of Botswana, northern Namibia and southern Angola, but they left evidence of their former extensive area of occupation throughout the sub-continent in rock paintings and engravings.

Between 2,000 and 3,000 years ago it appears that some hunter–gatherers in the region of northern Botswana acquired livestock, possibly as a result of contact with farmers further north, and turned to herding. The result of this 'pastoralist revolution' was that the herders, referred to as Khoikhoi, moved south in search of grazing land for their sheep and cattle. Although there is uncertainty as to the precise directions taken, likely moves were first into western Zimbabwe, the Transvaal and the Orange River tributaries, and then a split in which some continued south to the Cape coast and westward along the coastal plains of the southern Cape, while others moved along the Orange to the Atlantic coast and then south towards the Cape (Elphick and Malherbe 1989: 5). It was these Khoikhoi pastoralists that the Dutch encountered when they settled in the western Cape in the late seventeenth century.

Long before the Dutch arrival another major transformation had taken place within South Africa. Between AD 300 and 1000 crop cultivators moved into the region, some of whom also mined and processed metals such as copper and iron. Again the precise origins and directions of movement of these Iron Age cultivators are uncertain, but evidence from pottery artefacts indicates that they arrived in several streams from East and Central Africa, some penetrating the east coastal regions from Mozambique into Natal and others moving from Zimbabwe into the Transvaal and continuing into the Natal and Zululand interior and Transkei. Linguistic studies suggest that they were Bantu-speaking, unlike the Khoisan hunter–gatherers and pastoralists.

Iron Age settlements have been discovered over a wide area of the Transvaal, Natal, the Highveld and the eastern Cape. After *c*.1000 (a period known as the Late Iron Age) there was considerable expansion of the earlier Iron Age communities, particularly in the region of the Transvaal and Orange Free State highveld. It appears that cattle-keeping was becoming increasingly important to the cultivators and that the search for grazing land may have led to this extension of settlement. There is evidence of wide trading contacts between communities, some of which extended into the network of the flourishing Mapungubwe and Zimbabwe polities to the north. Control over trading goods and livestock also led to diversification of wealth and status within Iron Age communities. Small-scale polities under the control of those who dominated trade and cattle ownership were emerging. Although the details are far from clear, pre-colonial South African societies were certainly not static nor were they egalitarian (Hall 1987: 61–72).

Most such societies shared a structure of homestead-based pastoral and arable production, linked together in clans and presided over by a chief. Segmentation of this structure led to gradual dispersal and expansion of these polities. In some cases chiefdoms expanded their authority and developed into more centralized kingdoms or states. By the eighteenth century a number of such communities existed. In the interior most of these polities were of Sotho–Tswana speakers, one of which, the Pedi, had broken away from other Tswana formations and migrated further east. On the region between the Indian Ocean coast and the Drakensberg, Nguni-speaking descendants of Iron Age people had also evolved chiefdoms by the late seventeenth and eighteenth centuries, such as the Xhosa in the south and the Zulu in the north. They were still subject to considerable segmentation, as well as complex interaction with each other and with Khoi and San communities.

Both expansions, the Khoikhoi pastoralist and the Bantu-speaking arable, encroached on the hunting grounds of the San who were forced to retreat into areas less environmentally suited to livestock keeping and farming, such as the mountainous regions of the Drakensberg in Natal and the eastern Transvaal and the Cederberg of the western Cape. Contacts between Khoikhoi herders and cultivator communities were marked by the exchange of goods, although there were also conflicts over grazing lands for cattle. Thus the region had become both socially complex and economically diverse before colonial settlers moved in.

Colonial expansion at the Cape

1652 is etched into South African historical tradition as the date of the 'beginning of South Africa' because in that year the Dutch East

7

India Company (VOC) established a fort at Table Bay. But this was merely one community amongst many in South Africa. There is, therefore, the danger of over-stressing its significance. Yet the Cape colony that emerged from this early settlement was in the long term to provide the basis of the later colonial conquest of South Africa. The roots of that process require examination.

The VOC did not plan to acquire a large colony at the Cape. Settlers were initially only permitted to farm in order to provide the Company outpost and ships en route between the East Indies and Europe with essential foodstuffs. But by the end of the seventeenth century grain production had developed on an extensive arable basis and wine was also being cultivated, immigrants from Europe were settling on the land and colonial pastoralists were steadily encroaching on the grazing lands of Khoikhoi herders. Slave labour was imported from elsewhere in Africa, India and the East Indies to work on the settler farms, and a small urban community was developing around the fort and harbour in Cape Town.

By the early eighteenth century grazing permits were being issued for a small fee and the VOC guaranteed the rights of settlers to graze livestock on lands outside the original settled area as well as to cultivate them. Although immigration of further settlers was not encouraged after 1717, the colonial population grew rapidly in the eighteenth century as a result of high fertility rates and large family sizes (Ross 1975). Land could be obtained from the VOC for private use and could be sold or passed on to heirs. Property rights over land were thus entrenched by Company-backed law.

This led to increasing expansion of settler farming to the north and east of the Table Bay settlement. During the eighteenth century colonial stock farmers penetrated north into the region of the Land van Waveren (Tulbagh), the Bokkeveld and the Roggeveld, and eastwards to Swellendam and beyond. Extensive areas of land were being marked off for cattle and sheep grazing. Some farmers undoubtedly profited from the production of meat, wax and tallow and they maintained close links to the Cape Town market (Newton-King 1987). Others lacked sufficient capital to establish themselves as arable farmers in the western districts of the colony and appear to have been forced into pastoralism by economic necessity (Guelke 1989). Certainly by the early eighteenth century a complex settler society had emerged at the Cape with major disparities of wealth and status amongst the colonists.

This expansion of pastoralism was the first phase of colonial territorial conquest in South Africa. The regions occupied by the trekboer settlers were the grazing lands of Khoikhoi herders. From as early as 1659 conflict between the Dutch and the Khoikhoi was endemic. A series of raids for cattle by both parties, confrontations and uneasy truces marked the whole period of VOC rule at the Cape. In the 1670s the Khoi of the Cape Peninsula and its hinterland were defeated in a series of VOC raids, lost their cattle and were reduced to tributary status. From then on some Khoi began to work alongside imported slaves as labourers on the settler farms, a clear sign of their loss of economic independence.

To the north Khoi were denied access to grazing and water resources and in some cases were robbed of cattle by settler commandos. There is clear evidence that by the early eighteenth century some pastoralists were reduced to the hunter–gatherer existence of the San. In the late 1730s there was a protracted period of guerrilla resistance by the Khoi and San against settler farmers, and the VOC was only able to re-establish control over the region by condoning settler theft of Khoi cattle and sending a major commando to the area. From the 1770s to c.1800 conflict over environmental resources again broke out between trekkers, Khoi and San as colonial farmers penetrated further inland. As a result the armed trekboer commando became more firmly established, both to combat Khoi and San opposition and to capture women and children who were used as indentured labourers. Settler control was also extended over indigenous labourers by such devices as the enforced carrying of passes by 'Bastaard Hottentots' (the offspring of Khoi and slaves or Khoi and colonists). As a result of these conflicts and controls numerous Khoi, San and escaped slaves were fleeing to Namaqualand and the Orange River region by the late eighteenth century, where they formed communities known as the Oorlams. At the same time, guerrilla type resistance continued in the mountains of the Bokkeveld and Roggeveld (Penn 1989).

There was less overt confrontation between Khoi and those trekboers who were expanding eastwards parallel to the south Cape coast, although there is evidence that Khoi pastoralists were being steadily pushed back towards the Karoo and Camdeboo regions. By the 1770s settler farming had penetrated the rich grazing lands between the Gamtoos and Fish rivers which were also being used by Xhosa herders and cultivators. In 1786 the VOC formally extended the colony to this region with the establishment of a landdrost (magistracy) at Graaff-Reinet. As in the north, some Khoi and San were captured for indentured labour on settler farms, while others were reduced to

9

working for the trekkers as herders because they had lost access to cattle and pasturage (Newton-King and Malherbe 1981). Isolated episodes of resistance and guerrilla attacks on both Xhosa and settler farms took place, but it was not until 1799 that a major rebellion broke out when Khoi and San servants deserted the farms and began a four-year war aiming to reclaim the 'country of which our fathers have been despoiled' (Elphick and Malherbe 1989: 33).

In several ways the 1799–1803 rebellion differed significantly from earlier Khoi and San resistance. Firstly it was an uprising by those who had already lost the means of an independent existence, worked for the trekboers and aimed to overthrow settler society from within rather than simply to stem its territorial expansion. Moreover the rebels made common cause with Xhosa chiefs who were resisting colonial advances in the region with considerable success. The threat that this posed to the colonial order led to decisive intervention by the new colonial rulers who had taken over control of the Cape from the VOC: the British and, for a brief interlude, the Dutch Batavian administration.

The last years of VOC rule had witnessed a weak and financially bankrupt administration attempting unsuccessfully to control frontier conflicts with the Xhosa. In addition they had been faced by a declaration of an independent republic by settler 'Patriots' in Swellendam and Graaff-Reinet who resented restrictive VOC economic controls and demanded firmer action against the Xhosa. The first British and Batavian administrations attempted to minimize their costs and although they overcame the Patriots by an effective embargo on ammunition and other goods they were only prepared, or able, to enforce uneasy truces with the Xhosa, the Khoisan and the eastern district colonists.

After the permanent establishment of British control in 1806 more decisive action was taken. The need to keep costs low and to minimize internal conflicts led the British government into close alliance with local Dutch administrators. In a clear resolve to minimize potential conflict with settler farmers firm intervention against the Xhosa took place. Competition between settlers and Xhosa chiefdoms for pasturage in the regions west of the Zuurveld grew in the first decade of the nineteenth century. In 1811 the new Cape Governor, Sir John Cradock, ordered a major armed force of British, settler and loyal Khoi troops into the region. The army ruthlessly attacked the Xhosa, capturing their cattle and deliberately exercising no restraint. As Cradock reported to the Colonial Office in London in March of

10

1812, 'there has not been shed more Kaffir blood than would seem to be necessary to impress on the minds of these savages a proper degree of terror and respect' (Maclennan 1986: ix). Although further conflict took place in the 1810s, the uncertain balance between settlers and Xhosa in the Zuurveld frontier was decisively shifted in favour of the colony by British military intervention.

In the aftermath of these conflicts the leader of the campaign, Colonel Graham, proposed that Highland crofters, then being evicted from their homes in Scotland, be encouraged to settle in the Zuurveld. This proposal came to nothing but it prefigured the settlement schemes of the early 1820s by which British immigrants were brought to the region. The purpose was twofold: to relieve population pressure, poverty and endemic civil disorder at home and to assert control by the Cape colony over previously contested land in South Africa. Many of the new immigrants failed as farmers and moved into the villages and small towns of the colony. Clashes between Xhosa and colonists over land and cattle continued into the 1830s, but the eastern frontier had been effectively brought under settler control. The first stage of colonial conquest of the land was over. A new phase soon followed.

Settler dispersal

The first half of the nineteenth century was marked by more hesitant colonial expansion than before at the Cape. The British administration focused on attempting to make the colony pay its own way rather than expanding its boundaries. The most significant changes came to the internal ordering of the colony. The incorporation of the Cape into the empire of an industrializing Britain led to a move away from the tied labour systems of the earlier period towards a more mobile, though no less impoverished, labour force. Restrictions on Khoi labour were lifted in 1828 and slavery was abolished in the following decade. At the same time the focus of the economy shifted away from the arable western districts. Merchant houses in Cape Town and later Port Elizabeth, backed by British capital, provided loans and credit to enable some farmers to expand their market links, especially with the development of merino sheep wool production. This transformed the economy of the central and eastern Cape from the 1830s, leading to the emergence of a capitalizing farmer gentry,

11

the increasing value of land and the extrusion of labour tenants (Crais 1986).

These developments led to the migration out of the colony of about 15,000 eastern Cape pastoralists in the 1830s. This 'Great Trek' came to be seen in the twentieth century as the seminal event in South African history when it provided the symbolic images crucial to the ethos of Afrikaner nationalism. Perhaps because of this it has until recently received little attention from historians other than those writing in an Afrikaner nationalist tradition. Certainly the Trek differed both in scale and intent from the trekboer migrations of the preceding century. The trekkers complained in particular against the failure of the colonial administration to grant them representative government and the social implications of placing freed slaves and Khoi servants 'on an equal footing with Christians, contrary to the laws of God and the natural distinction of race and colour' (Muller 1975: 154).

But outrage at the apparent subversion of the social order by the colonial government was not the only cause of the Great Trek. As Peires (1989) has shown, economic impoverishment played an important role. The trekkers were not members of the new capitalizing wool gentry and many of them still rented land from the state. They were adversely affected by the Cape government's attempt to regularize land tenure since many of them were heavily in arrears on rent payments and thus unable to acquire legal ownership. They were also disadvantaged by the recent devaluation of the rixdollar. Although the economic position of the trekkers still requires a full analysis, certainly some, such as the leader Piet Retief, were heavily in debt and were being pursued by creditors. Leaving the Cape thus had decided individual advantages. Etherington (1991) has also pointed out that land speculation was a likely motive for the trekkers, who were aiming a 'pre-emptive strike' against the merchant houses of the Cape by claiming land in Natal for profitable resale value.

The trek was not a movement in constant opposition to African polities, as some traditional interpretations maintain. Louis Tregardt, a key trekker leader, headed first for land owned by the Xhosa king Hintsa. The two developed a relationship of mutual advantage: in return for land Tregardt provided Hintsa with firearms (Peires 1989: 506–7). Further conflict between the Xhosa and the Cape colonists in the late 1830s ended this symbiotic relationship between Hintsa and the trekkers. However, it is an important warning against seeing the penetration of the Voortrekkers into the interior as the steady march of a racially conscious 'volk' seeking to establish themselves in the 'empty land' away from colonial or African control. Conflict, co-operation and complex interaction between and amongst trekkers and others marked the history of mid-nineteenth-century South Africa.

As we have already noted the interior of South Africa was by no means an empty land. It was, however, undergoing a period of major transformation. Since the 1960s historians have recognized that a process at least as significant as the Great Trek was taking place within the African polities of the sub-continent. Known as the Mfecane (Nguni) or Difaqane (Sotho), it involved the consolidation and expansion of the Zulu kingdom in the Natal lowveld in the 1820s, the subsequent migration of other Nguni-speaking people into the highveld and the often violent competition for land and livestock with the inhabitants of those areas. Dispersal and reformation of chiefdoms took place over a wide area and as a result new polities, such as the Sotho, the Swazi and the Ndebele, emerged while others, such as the Pedi and Tswana, expanded and reformed. The process was believed to have been cataclysmic and highly destructive (Omer-Cooper 1966).

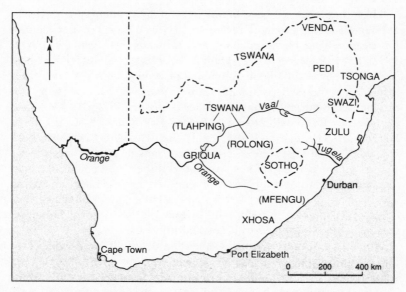

Map 1 African societies in the nineteenth century *Source*: adapted from J. Pampallis, 1991: *Foundations of the new South Africa*, Cape Town: Maskew Miller Longman; London: Zed Books, 4.

13

The precise causes of the Mfecane are less clear. Some writers have argued that it resulted from the particular military skills and social reorganization of the Zulu king Shaka in the early 1820s, others that it was the outcome of longer-term environmental impoverishment of the northern Natal region (Gluckman 1960; Guy 1980). Such theories of internal causes of change have consciously rejected as Eurocentric the interpretation that the Zulu were able to spread into their neighbours' grazing lands because they had external links with traders from Delagoa Bay (Smith 1969).

More recently, however, Cobbing has suggested that outside pressures were indeed fundamental, but that they took the form of demands for labour. The eastern Cape looked to the Orange, Highveld and Drakensberg regions and the Portuguese slave-trading network centred on Delagoa Bay drew on the Mfolosi and Tugela regions. Such pressures were building up before the 1810s when the 'internal revolution' of the Mfecane is believed to have begun. Cobbing believes that the whole concept of the Mfecane was developed by contemporaries to disguise the real roots of dislocation which were the slaving activities of colonists both to the north and to the south (1988).

These new theories have found some support amongst historians, although Cobbing has more recently also been accused of over-stating his case, relying on speculation and misusing evidence (Saunders 1992: 83–4; Eldredge 1992; Hamilton 1992). Eldredge (1992) has argued that low rainfall, environmental disruption and food shortages throughout the sub-continent caused increased competition for productive resources amongst southern African societies which was exploited by Cape colonists and Delagoa Bay traders in their search for labour. The debate has certainly pointed to the need to look beyond Natal alone in the search for the roots of the changes of the 1820s, but the precise connections between these and colonial labour demand are still uncertain and Cobbing's apparent denial of African agency is unpopular amongst those who see the actions of Shaka and other key figures of the Mfecane as examples of African initiatives which had nothing to do with colonial influences.

Whatever the outcome of the Mfecane debate it is certainly true that colonial influences were felt outside the boundaries of the Cape colony before the Great Trek. For instance, from the early nineteenth century ivory and hide hunters and traders who were agents of Cape merchants had established a small coastal settlement at Port Natal (later Durban), which owed nominal allegiance to the Zulu state. A party of Voortrekkers arrived in 1838 and formed an alliance with the traders and some disaffected African cultivators in the region. Together they defeated the Zulu under Dingane at the battle of Blood River, declared a new Republic of Natalia and claimed rights to the land between the Tukela and Mzimkulu rivers. Their numbers were small and land was occupied by Africans, many of whom moved into the region after Dingane's defeat. Land speculation was rife, however, and a pattern of large-scale land ownership by settlers with African 'squatter' cultivation emerged (Slater 1980).

In 1843 Natalia was annexed by the British in a wave of humanitarian outrage at reports of trekker use of slaves, but also in an attempt to stem Nguni migration further south which could disrupt the precarious eastern Cape frontier. Many of the Voortrekkers left as a result but merchants and traders continued to speculate in land in the hope that a commercial boom encouraged by immigrant British farmers would increase its value. Natal's future as a colony of white settlement was thus established. About 5,000 immigrants arrived between 1849 and 1852 under a variety of colonization schemes, most from Britain but some from Germany and others from Mauritius. Commercial penetration from the Cape and Britain swiftly followed, although early hopes of cotton and coffee booms were disappointed. Maize, wool and stock farming took root but it was not until the mid-1850s that sugar began to be cultivated along the Natal coast. Large-scale commercial plantations emerged closely allied with the interests of Cape merchants and, from the 1860s, dependent on indentured labour from India (Richardson 1986; Ballard 1989).

Elsewhere the trekkers also depended both on local alliances in the aftermath of the Mfecane and on commercial links with colonial agents. Some crossed the Vaal River and attempted to establish settlements in the eastern Transvaal with links to Delagoa Bay. However, internal fragmentation, inability to obtain grazing land from the Pedi, Swazi and Tsonga cultivators of the region and depletion of hunting stock led to further settler dispersion. In the Soutpansberg region of the northern Transvaal highveld, trekkers engaged in ivory hunting from the late 1830s with the aid of Venda huntsmen and traded the products to the Delagoa Bay market in exchange for manufactured goods, guns and ammunition. These hunters also raided the surrounding areas for slaves and depended upon forced indentured labour. However, their fragility was marked by their inability to survive in competition for resources with Venda and Tsonga hunters by the 1860s (Wagner 1980).

The strongest trekker community in the Transvaal centred on Potchefstroom. Land had been settled here in the aftermath of Ndebele migration northwards from the area, and some of the trekkers from Natal joined in 1848. Its independence as the 'South African Republic' was assured after the British accepted the principle of Boer independence north of the Vaal River at the Sand River Convention of 1852. It was, however, still dependent on trading contacts with the Cape, particularly in firearms and ammunition which were used against local Tswana communities to obtain tributary indentured labour.

In the highveld south of the Vaal trekkers also became involved in complex alliances and conflicts in the aftermath of the Mfecane. They were aided by the Rolong of Thaba Nchu in their conflict with the Ndebele in 1836–7, and together they penetrated deep into the western Transvaal, where some settled on lands which were later joined to the South African Republic, in pursuit of the Ndebele. Further to the east trekkers had been buying or renting land from the Griqua (themselves descendants of migrants from the Cape in the late eighteenth century) and also competing with the Sotho polity under Moshoeshoe for grazing pastures between the Caledon and Orange rivers. Cattle raiding and skirmishes were endemic in the area throughout the 1840s, disrupting lines of trade north of the Cape and raising the spectre of a powerful Sotho kingdom on the borders of the colony.

In 1848 the Cape Governor, Sir Harry Smith, declared the annexation of the region between the Orange and the Vaal rivers as the 'Orange River Sovereignty', and a British army defeated resistance of the trekkers under Pretorius and imposed a strict boundary on Sotho cultivation and pastorage. Tension between the Sotho and the British ensued, and Moshoeshoe inflicted some defeats on them and appealed for trekker support from north of the Vaal. It was in return for a promise of trekker neutrality in this dangerous situation that the British conceded Boer independence in the Transvaal (or the South African Republic as it became known) in 1852.

Further Sotho resistance to British attacks led to a truce and colonial withdrawal from the region. By the Bloemfontein Convention of 1854 the trekkers gained theoretical control of most of the territory, renamed the Orange Free State. But as with the South African Republic in the Transvaal, the Free State was still dependent on trading links with the Cape, particularly in guns and ammunition, and the government lacked the ability to enforce control over the land they officially occupied. Sotho assertion of grazing and cultivation rights meant that settler control remained nominal.

The mid-nineteenth century is sometimes seen as a period of colonial retreat from the South African interior. In the case of formal British rule this was certainly true of the early 1850s in the Transvaal and Free State regions. Yet withdrawal here had little to do with loss of interest in the interior. Armed resistance, by both trekkers and Africans, sometimes in alliance, had played a part in withdrawal. But by this time the British at the Cape realized that they had little to gain from costly conquest and direct administration over such extensive regions inhabited by conflicting polities. Trade in ivory, skins and maize was firmly directed towards the Cape, and migrant labourers, particularly Tswana and Pedi, had come to the colony from at least the 1840s (Delius 1980; Kinsman 1983). Considerable colonial economic influence, if not direct political control, was thus well established by the 1850s.

Where Cape economic interests were threatened, however, the British did not hesitate to intervene. By the 1840s wool farmers and merchants in the eastern Cape were calling for the expansion of grazing lands into the Ciskei region. In 1846, the Cape Governor Maitland ordered an attack on the Xhosa of the region on the pretext that one of them, who was accused of stealing an axe, had been rescued from Fort Beaufort jail and a police officer killed in the process. In fact the 'War of the Axe' was about land control and it unleashed a new period of Cape–Xhosa confrontation (Peires 1981: 134–60). A scorched earth policy by the British led to the occupation of the region, now declared as 'British Kaffraria'. A Xhosa counter-attack in 1850 was joined by eastern Cape Khoi from mission stations and farm labourers who feared expulsion and encroachment from capitalizing wool farmers (Kirk 1980). The result was what Crais has described as 'a class war' (1986: 140). Fears that it would spread also caused widespread panic in the western districts of the colony. Although they were unfounded they indicate the tensions which existed in the colony and which were expressed in firmer labour controls after the Cape achieved a measure of self-government in 1854 (Bradlow 1989).

In the aftermath of this devastation a millenarian movement arose amongst the Xhosa. A teenage girl, Nongqawuse, prophesied that Xhosa self-purification by destruction of their own crops and cattle would lead to intervention by the ancestors to rid them of the colonial

17

forces and to re-establish prosperity. Peires has shown that these ideas cannot be characterized simply as superstitious pagan reactions to colonial rule. The idea of cattle killing was evoked by a crippling epidemic of lungsickness which destroyed over 100,000 Xhosa cattle in 1854. Moreover, the notion of the rising ancestors owed much to Christian missionary teachings about the resurrection and afterlife which had infiltrated the region. Peires concludes that 'the central beliefs of the Xhosa cattle killing were neither irrational nor atavistic. Ironically it was because they were so rational and so appropriate that they ultimately proved to be so deadly' (1987: 63). The logic of Nongqawuse's prophecy led to widespread obedience to her instructions.

Only those chiefs (about 15 per cent of the total) who had made individual benefits from the opportunities provided by the colonial presence failed to back the prophecy. So the subsequent famine and disillusionment with the loyal chiefs of the old order led to fatal weaknesses in the Xhosa polity (Peires 1986). As a result full colonial occupation of the Ciskei region took place, pre-colonial Xhosa society west of the Kei River was destroyed and local chiefs were subordinated to British magistrates. British Kaffraria was subsequently annexed to the Cape in 1866.

In comparison with other colonies such as those in Australia and Canada, the rate of European immigration to the Cape by the mid-nineteenth century was still very slow. Its impact was also less complete. By the 1860s settler dispersal from the Cape had been accompanied by colonial trading and military and political intervention. But although direct British conquest had taken place in the eastern Cape, Ciskei and Natal, a large degree of trekker and African independence from colonial control still existed. Also, the balance of power in the interior had not by any means shifted to the trekker Boers, and in both the South African Republic and the Orange Free State African chiefdoms and states exerted control over land and trade. Notable polities such as the Zulu kingdom in northern Natal and the Pedi state in the eastern Transvaal remained little affected by settler penetration. In the coming decades, however, this situation was to change dramatically.

Colonial conquest

In the 1850s, the British appeared to withdraw from direct political control over the South African interior. But from the 1870s they

18

adopted an aggressive thrust into the whole sub-continent. In the course of two decades Basutoland, Griqualand West, the South African Republic in the Transvaal, the Transkei and Bechuanaland were conquered and the Zulu and Pedi were defeated and their lands brought under imperial control. The British did not have everything their own way; there were major setbacks when they were defeated by the Zulu and they were forced to withdraw from the Transvaal. But clearly their policy had become direct and interventionist and it fundamentally changed the map of South Africa. What brought about this change?

Prior to the 1970s two kinds of explanations existed. According to an early argument set out by the liberal writer de Kiewiet (1937), the British drive to unify the region under their control was motivated by the belief that integration was a rational and evolutionary step towards civilization and progress and was fuelled by humanitarian concern at the treatment of Africans in the trekker republics. Other historians stressed that the new thrust inland was part of the wider scramble for empire, particularly in Africa, amongst European powers. Anxious to prevent their rivals from gaining access to the trade of the interior, the British pushed for direct control. Alternative variants of this argument stress the British need to protect their vital naval base at Simonstown, near Cape Town, and to secure their sea route to India (Goodfellow 1966) or that local crises propelled them inland (Robinson and Gallagher 1961).

While there is no doubt that European power rivalry and heightened colonial competition were a vital broad background to the expansion of direct British rule in South Africa, more recent work has stressed the significance of factors particular to the region. In an influential article published in 1974, Atmore and Marks pointed to the crucial significance of the discovery of diamonds on the Vaal-Hartz river junction in 1867, the rush to the Kimberley diamond fields and the massive growth of mining that followed. The discovery of valuable mineral deposits and the need to secure labour supplies to mine them made the South African interior a highly desirable region for the British to control directly. It was also apparent that none of the existing polities, including the Cape, possessed either the will or the ability to deal with the demands of the mining industry, particularly their need for transport infrastructure and labour. Furthermore the Colonial Office received complaints that the Transvaal government was inhibiting the free flow of labour to the diamond fields as well as to the farms and plantations of the Cape and Natal by pass laws

19

enacted in 1873 and 1874. Direct control over the highveld would thus enable a variety of settler and colonial interests to secure and regulate African labour.

More recent work has fully vindicated this argument and has fleshed out some of the details. Etherington (1979) showed that between 1874 and 1878 Carnarvon, the British Colonial Secretary, was directly influenced by Theophilus Shepstone, Natal's Secretary for Native Affairs, to push for a federation of the South African colonies and republics under British sovereignty. Shepstone and the Natal settlers who backed him were influenced not only by the needs of the diamond mines but also by reports of gold deposits in the eastern Transvaal. They also noted with alarm the diversion of migrant labourers from the eastern Transvaal and Mozambique away from Natal as a result of Transvaal government interference. Natal planters in particular showed great interest in expansion further north, ostensibly to suppress the East African and Portuguese slave trade but also to secure access themselves to labourers, albeit wage labourers, from these regions. The Transvaal Republic as well as the Zulu kingdom stood in the way of such schemes. At the same time officials in the diamond fields were also stressing the need to protect the migrant labour route from the north, especially from the Pedi, which trekker commandos in the Transvaal were raiding for their own labour supplies.

Cope supports this view and points out that there is no reason to doubt that Carnarvon's intentions behind the confederation were

> to replace the existing categories of weak, poor and unprogressive states by a single strong and efficient state possessing the credit and security for enterprise necessary to develop the country, and to bring to an end the political and economic independence of the Africans and incorporate them as the working class of this economically and geographically expanding new dominion, which would be a source of strength to the empire.

> (1986: 16)

There is no sign that Carnarvon was concerned about the security of naval bases or that he had philanthropic desires to protect Africans. On the contrary, although he was opposed to slavery and coerced labour, he was strongly influenced by the failure of the post-

20

emancipation plantation economy of Jamaica which lacked the means of channelling freed slaves into wage labour, and he believed that securing an adequate supply of African wage labour was essential to British interests in South Africa (Cope 1989). Where obstacles to this existed, from either African or Boer polities, the colonial power intervened.

It is against this background that the events of the 1870s and 1880s should be viewed. Soon after the discovery of the diamond fields the British moved to pre-empt attempts by the Boer republics to divide the region between them by backing both Thlaping and Griqua claims to the area and annexing it as Griqualand West to 'protect' the Griqua from Boer encroachment. The Thlaping inhabitants of the colony were squeezed by the inrush of diamond prospectors, land speculators and colonial officials to whom they lost valuable grazing land. Some profited by the opportunities of arable production for the Kimberley mines but Thlaping rights of land ownership were further undermined by British backing of Griqua claims. In 1878 some Thlaping chiefs together with some Griqua and San rebelled against colonial rule in the territory. As a result their cattle were confiscated and they were confined to rural locations and obliged to pay hut taxes to the authorities.

Griqualand West was handed over to the Cape colony in 1880, but British expansion in the region continued with the annexation of southern Bechuanaland in 1884–5, ostensibly to resist Transvaal occupation of part of the area but in fact to secure vital areas of timber, grain and labour supply to Kimberley. In 1895 this region was also annexed to the Cape, then under the premiership of the mining magnate Cecil Rhodes whose ambitions lay in trading and mineral expansion further to the north. By then a combination of factors – the intensifying encroachment of settler stock farms and railway building on the land, hut taxes which undermined chiefly authority and control over tribute and the culling of cattle affected by rinderpest all combined to lead to increasing Thlaping impoverishment and discontent. In 1896 a revolt in the Langeberg region was suppressed. The leaders were imprisoned, many of their followers indentured as labourers and the land was confiscated. The last vestiges of southern Tswana autonomy were destroyed (Shillington 1985).

The experiences of the Tswana were paralleled by those of other polities further away from the diamond mines. In the Transvaal the Boers staked a claim to land under the aegis of the Pedi kingdom, with aid from the Swazi polity further east, but they were unable to enforce it and had to provide tribute to the Pedi to obtain access to their labour. Attempts in the late 1860s to collect rents and taxes from other Africans residing on land claimed by Boers met with opposition and increasing migration to the protection of the Pedi (Delius 1983: 126–57). In 1869 Sekhukhune, the Pedi chief, overcame a Swazi attack in support of a rival claimant to his power and in the early 1870s he began to expand grazing and cultivation on Boer-claimed land in the Lydenburg region, where small-scale gold mining had been started by white prospectors. Other Pedi from mission stations and Boer farms moved to join the expanding polity in a search for land denied to them by missionaries and settlers. Conflict resulted from rising competition for land and labour resources as the market for both increased with the expansion of diamond mining at Kimberley and the possibilities of gold discoveries in the eastern Transvaal. In 1876 forces of the South African Republic attacked Sekhukhune and demanded tribute, but were repelled in several skirmishes.

It was in this context that in 1877 Shepstone annexed the Transvaal on behalf of the British, a move made easier by the defeat of the republic in conflict with the Pedi. This was a vital part of Carnarvon's federation policy, supported both by the Lydenburg miners and the mercantile and banking sectors of the Transvaal who welcomed access to a confederated South Africa but opposed by many Boer farmers. Yet Shepstone immediately bolstered settler claims to land and demanded war indemnity and hut taxes from the Pedi. Sekhukhune's inability to provide this at a time of drought and cattle shortage, and Shepstone's fears that the Pedi would resist British land claims, led to a major attack in 1879 with Swazi support and the defeat of the Pedi paramountcy. The Pedi had stood in the way of colonial land and labour policy and paid the cost. The conquest of the Pedi was final and subjugation of the region continued after the re-establishment of Boer control over the Transvaal in 1881.

The British attack on the Pedi came in the immediate wake of defeat of another major African polity, the Zulu state. Natal settlers had long resented their inability to extract labour from the Zulu kingdom, which had forced sugar planters to employ indentured Indian workers. There were also fears of a growing African presence in the colony. In 1873 mild defiance of Shepstone by the Hlubi chief Langalibalele had led to a violent retribution by the Natal government of crop burning, killing and land seizure. The Zulu were less easily subdued and the Natal colony had entered an uneasy alliance which recognized the Zulu state under Cetshwayo and supported its territorial claims against the South African Republic. After British annexation of the Transvaal, the position changed. Shepstone laid claims to disputed territory between the Transvaal and Zululand, an important corridor for migrant labour from the north. In addition Frere, the British High Commissioner, seeing the Zulu state as a major barrier to confederation, gathered troops in Natal and accused Cetshwayo of cattle raiding. When in 1879 the Zulu refused to accept a British Resident or the disbanding of their army, British forces invaded Zululand. After a catastrophic defeat at Isandlwana, which terrified the Natalians by revealing that colonial forces were not invincible, massive reinforcements finally defeated the Zulu at Ulundi. Peace was arranged by which Cetshwayo was exiled to Cape Town and Zululand was divided into smaller chiefdoms under the control of those who had little traditional authority.

Hopes of a more pliable situation in which taxes and labour could at last be extracted were frustrated by the ensuing civil conflict. In an attempt to bring about peace the British restored Cetshwayo and partitioned Zululand, but conflicts between different chiefdoms, Natal settlers and Transvaal Boers continued. Finally in 1887 the British asserted direct control over a large part of Zululand which was incorporated into Natal in 1897. The rest was ceded to the Transvaal.

The destruction of the Zulu kingdom led to a fundamental restructuring of Zulu society. While homestead production under chiefly administration was retained, the British demanded hut taxes in place of the military service or tribute previously granted to the king and encouraged labour recruitment for the mines of the Rand and the farms and plantations of Natal. By the late 1880s, the Zulu were becoming enmeshed in the migrant labour system (Guy 1982). After annexation to Natal, heavier tax and labour demands, crop seizures and land destruction led to final Zulu resistance in the Bambatha rebellion of 1906–8. Described by Marks as a peasant rebellion which marked 'the last armed resistance to proletarianisation by Africans' (1986b: 351), it raised the spectre to the British and the Natalians of a revived Zulu threat. The rebels lacked the resources to combat the greatly strengthened colonial state in Natal, and were ruthlessly crushed.

The defeat of the Tswana, Pedi and Zulu polities by the British was also accompanied in this period by colonial control over areas bordering on the Cape Colony in which the Cape government had intervened. In 1878 Frere invaded the Transkeian territories after Cape intervention in a dispute between the Mfengu and Xhosa. In the course of the early 1880s these were initially placed under the indirect administration of colonial-appointed magistrates and were then formally annexed. Only the Pondoland region remained outside direct settler control, but this too was incorporated into the Cape Colony in the subsequent decade. At the same time attacks were made on the Sotho polity in which it was believed that arms obtained with the wages of migrant workers were being accumulated. Refusal to pay taxes and cede their guns to the Cape administration led to war in 1880, but the Cape forces were unable to bring the Sotho under their control. Subsequently Basutoland came under direct British 'protection'. Since labour was already forthcoming there was little point in treating the Sotho in the same way as the Zulu state, and local chiefs retained much of their authority.

By the end of the 1880s the British had effectively exerted control, either directly or through their colonies in the Cape and Natal, over a large number of African societies. They did not, however, achieve their goal of a South African Confederation. The major setback to this was Boer resistance in the Transvaal. After the defeat of the Pedi the need for armed forces in the Transvaal was removed, and a rebellion led by Boer farmers succeeded in defeating the British occupiers. After final defeat at Majuba in 1881, the British agreed to withdraw.

These events marked a significant growth of Afrikaner nationalism and resentment at continued British influence in the region. It also led to a strengthened republican state in the Transvaal under President Kruger which in the 1880s and 1890s was able to assert much more direct control over Africans in the region. Assaults on the Ndebele in the east, the Rolong Tswana in the west and the Venda of the Soutpansberg in the north led to effective Boer control over the Transvaal. In addition the Swazi kingdom in the east was weakened in the 1880s by its policy of granting concessions to external agents for such items as grazing rights, minerals and timber (Bonner 1983: 160–207). This region then became the focus of Boer attempts to gain access to the coast from the Transvaal and equal British determination to prevent them. In 1895, despite Swazi protests, the area was placed under the protectorate of Kruger's government in return for an agreement from the Transvaal not to intervene north of the Limpopo. In a final act of land control, the British then annexed Tongaland, north of Natal, to cut off Boer access to the sea.

24

The process of conquest of African polities in the last three decades of the nineteenth century was the direct result of a more aggressive British imperial intervention, motivated by the need to secure labour for the mines and plantations and to benefit from the increased economic potential of the sub-continent. A variety of methods ranging from exploitation of internal conflicts, often in turn produced by colonial pressures, and direct armed confrontation to taxation and land seizure brought most Africans within the orbit of new economic and political forces. Resistance occurred at every stage, sometimes achieving a temporary reprieve but ultimately unable to stem the advance of colonial control. A final blow to those farmers who did retain some independence came with the rinderpest epidemic of 1896–7. This cattle disease swept through the sub-continent, reducing many herders to extreme poverty, in some cases starvation, and forcing others to seek work on settler farms or the mines. In the face of increasing colonial pressures many African farmers were unable to recover from the impact of the disease. It was a factor in the revolts in both Basutoland and Griqualand, both of which were swiftly put down (Van Onselen 1972).

Indigenous independence was thus largely destroyed but South Africa in the early 1890s was still divided into settler colonies and Boer republics. It took a major war between them before a unitary state could be established.

The South African War and Union

The South African (Anglo–Boer) War of 1899–1902 marked the completion of the process of conquest begun in the 1870s. The British conquest of the Transvaal and the Orange Free State during the war paved the way for the unification of a single South African state in 1910. There has been much debate about the causes of the war, some of which parallel the arguments over imperial aims in the 1870s and 1880s. Imperial rivalry with a growing Afrikaner nationalism in the Republics and with other European powers, especially Germany, defence of the sea route to India and the ambitions of particular individuals such as Chamberlain the Colonial Secretary, Rhodes the Cape Prime Minister, and Milner, the British High Commissioner, have all been evoked. Certainly these factors all played a role, but the essential catalyst now widely accepted by historians was undoubtedly economic. Whereas the conquests of the

25

1870s and 1880s were fuelled by the diamond discoveries, the South African War was caused by the second and major stage of the 'Mineral Revolution' – the development of gold mining on the Witwatersrand.

Atmore and Marks (1974) stressed the parallels between these two periods of decisive British intervention in South Africa. In both cases mineral discoveries and rapid mining investment brought demands for labour and infrastructure which the British believed existing polities could not meet or were obstructing. But a difference lay in the nature of the mineral mined. Gold was central to the fiscal stability of the capitalist world economy of the 1890s, since the currencies of many industrial nations were based on the gold standard. Gold production had fallen worldwide since the 1870s, and British financial interests, especially nervous after the 1890 crash of the Baring Brothers financiers, were concerned to secure control over the Rand gold supplies which by 1898 were the largest single source and accounted for 27.5 per cent of total world gold output (Richardson and Van-Helten 1980: 19). In 1899, on the eve of the war, gold supplies at the Bank of England were again falling.

Only by annexing Kruger's Transvaal and completing their control over the whole of South Africa, argued Marks and Trapido (1979), could the British secure the gold supplies and profits of the Rand and construct a state which would support the interests of the mining industry. By the late 1890s, it was apparent that the Transvaal had become the most economically valuable region of southern Africa. Rhodesia had been invaded and conquered by Cecil Rhodes's British South Africa Company in 1890, but hopes that it would become a 'second Rand' had proved unfounded. So without influence or direct control over the Transvaal, British economic and political paramountcy in southern Africa was impossible (Davenport 1991: 187).

Recently some attention has again been given to the political context of the decision by the British to push for war. Porter (1990) has questioned the extent to which Chamberlain or Milner were directly concerned with local mining magnates and whether war was in the best interests of the industry, while Smith (1990) emphasizes the British and Afrikaner rivalry stemming from the Transvaal conflicts of 1880–1. Conquest of the Transvaal in 1899 was only made essential because the Transvaal government was not one 'friendly' to, and prepared to collaborate with, British imperial interests. Control over the polity of the Transvaal as much as over the economy of the mining industry was crucial (Smith 1990: 59).

Whatever the precise differences of emphasis in these accounts, the Rand mining industry was nonetheless a vital component of the scenario which led to the South African War. The potential of the region was swiftly recognized after the initial gold discoveries in 1886. The initial rush led to speculation and collapse when the shallow level deposits were swiftly exhausted, but by 1895 deep level mining predominated. This required much greater capital investment, not only from the mining companies of the Kimberley fields but increasingly from Europe and especially Britain. It also required more complex technological equipment to mine the deep but thin veins of ore. High production costs, the need for costly immigrant skilled labour and the fixed price obtainable for the gold meant that mine owners could only obtain profits by recruiting cheap local unskilled labour, for which they required state support.

The mining industry was a major tax payer to the Transvaal republic. The Kruger government, having therefore much to gain from it, was less obstructive than many contemporaries, and more recent historians, have maintained. It promulgated legislation allowing for legal private ownership of claims, facilitated mining company amalgamations and permitted purchase of land by mining houses, although with some understandable restrictions on private control of water resources. The government was concerned to ensure that the mines did not monopolize employment of African labour to the detriment of Boer farmers, but as Harries (1986) has shown, it did agree to labour recruiting for the mines with the Portuguese administration of Mozambique and it policed a pass system which prevented both wage competition by mines seeking a mobile force and desertion of workers under contracts. The mines failed to obtain monopoly control over labour recruiting but they were content to work with independent recruiting agents provided labour was forthcoming. Before 1900 this was indeed the case (Jeeves 1975).

Yet the mining companies had frustrations. Direct taxes on their profits increased as did duties on imported goods such as machinery. The government maintained monopolies over items such as the dynamite needed for deep-level blasting and for railway construction which led to high transport tariffs. Furthermore the administrative capacity of the South African Republic was not always able to effectively enforce the legislation desired by the mine owners. Lacking access to political power themselves, since as uitlanders (outsiders) they were not enfranchised, there was little the mining magnates could do to remedy the situation from within.

27

Blainey (1965) argued that it was the deep-level mine owners in particular who plotted with Rhodes to topple the Kruger government in 1895. Arms to back an uitlander coup were smuggled into Johannesburg and Rhodes ordered a small force of troops from Bechuanaland under the command of L.S. Jameson to support it. But the 'Jameson raid' was a fiasco. The Johannesburg uprising failed to materialize and Jameson's troops were captured soon after entering the Transvaal. Blainey's argument that it was only the deep-level miners who backed the raid has been much debated, although it has been broadly supported by Mendelsohn who has shown that it was indeed those mining houses with heavier investments and longer-term interests in the future of the industry who backed the conspiracy to topple the Boer government and replace it by 'one more easily manipulated by the mining industry' (1980: 170).

The Jameson raid resolved none of the problems of the uitlanders but merely exacerbated tensions and brought the situation in the Transvaal to wider international attention. Whitehall recognized the dangers of allowing local initiatives without adequate planning, and Kruger tried to appease the mining industry by legislative support on the one hand but consolidated alliances with the Orange Free State and made approaches to the Germans and Portuguese on the other. The mine owners continued to stress the injustice of uitlander exclusion from political power. In 1897 Chamberlain appointed Milner, known for his hawkish expansionist goals and his dislike of Kruger, as Cape Governor and British High Commissioner in South Africa. The following year, British hopes that Kruger's power might be on the wane and that uitlander interests could be promoted were dashed by his overwhelming victory in a presidential election. This was followed by a rapid build-up of propaganda against Kruger and of troops in the Cape and Natal. It seemed that Milner was determined on a path of confrontation.

In an attempt to strike a pre-emptive blow before his forces were totally outnumbered, and refusing the alternative of ceding long-term electoral control to the uitlanders, Kruger declared war on the British with support from the Orange Free State, and Boer forces invaded Natal and the northern Cape in October of 1899.

Both the Boers and the British hoped that the war would be short and decisive. In the event it was drawn out over three years, was highly destructive of life, property and produce, and entrenched a bitterness between Boer and British which was to endure throughout the twentieth century. It created the spectre of almost half a million troops of one of the most powerful industrial nations on earth bogged down by the commandos and guerrilla forces of what the British had belittled as backward and incompetent Boer rural states. The war extended over a wide area. Initial Boer advances and victories in the northern Cape and Natal were only halted after the relief of lengthy sieges at Ladysmith, Kimberley and Mafeking. By mid-1900 massive troop reinforcements enabled the British to reverse the tide and they captured Bloemfontein, Johannesburg and Pretoria. Theoretically the Boer republics were conquered. But Boer guerrilla resistance continued over the next two years, penetrating deep into the Cape as well as outmanoeuvring the imperial troops in the republics. The British adopted scorched earth tactics, destroying Boer farms, crops and livestock and most notoriously imprisoning the families and servants of the farmers in concentration camps. Only with extensive British military control over the highveld were the guerrilla commandos forced to surrender by the signing of the Treaty of Vereeniging in May 1902.

The war had been immensely destructive of life and property. An estimated 22,000 British troops died, the majority from disease. Over 30,000 farmsteads in the republics and northern Cape were destroyed. About 26,000 Boer women and children and 14,000 African internees died in the concentration camps (Warwick 1980: 60–1). The war also led to divisions within communities and families which spread beyond the sphere of formal military or guerilla actions, particularly in the Cape. The South African War was a civil war rather than simply a conflict between an imperial army and a local population.

Both at the time and since writers have maintained that this was a 'white man's war'. More recently, however, the significance of the involvement of other South Africans in the conflict has been recognized. Warwick (1983) has shown the crucial role that they played, both as combatants, often with old scores to settle, and as messengers, scouts and transport drivers. For instance, the Tswana in the northern Cape and western Transvaal attacked Boer cattle and encampments as well as assisting the British during the siege of Mafeking, and Zulus raided Boer territory which had previously been annexed from Zululand and aided the British in tracking down guerrillas. The Pedi under Sekhukhune did likewise in the hopes of regaining lands lost to the South African Republic. And volunteers in the Transkei, impoverished when closure of the mines during the war cut off migrant labour, armed for defence against possible Boer attacks. In the northern Cape mission stations, cultivators resisted guerrilla raids, defended the Cape Town–Kimberley railway line and acted as transport drivers for the British forces (Nasson 1983, 1991). On the Rand black workers were drafted by both sides, although by the end of the war most were wage earners in British military employment.

The war caused equal suffering to whites and blacks; many Africans died during the hostilities and in the concentration camps and others lost cattle commandeered by both sides. Yet paradoxically this destructive war of conquest did see a partial rolling back of colonial encroachment on land and the possibility for some African cultivators to recover from losses they had sustained over the past decades. In the Transvaal there was direct reappropriation of Boer land and cattle by the Kgatla Tswana and general flouting of land tenancy restrictions (Krikler 1989). Elsewhere in the Orange Free State and Natal the destruction and desertion of Boer farms led to repossession by African farmers. Indeed the impact of these gains was felt immediately after the war when both white farmers and mine owners complained at their inability to obtain sufficient labour.

But this rolling back of settler land control was limited in extent and short-lived. As Marks and Trapido (1979) have stressed, the period of 'reconstruction' by Milner's conquest state in the Transvaal between the end of the war and 1905 was marked by an intensification of colonial control over land and labour and a process of 'social engineering' in the interests of a growing capitalist economy. The state provided cheap indentured labour from China which enabled the mines to lower wages and undercut African demands for higher pay and better working conditions (Richardson 1982). Land resettlement schemes returned Boer farmers to the land as well as introducing some British immigrants, but the Milner government opposed land tenancy arrangements for Africans and 'was determined to transform all black tenants into wage labourers' (Marks and Trapido 1979: 70). The Milner administration enforced these measures more efficiently than had been possible under Kruger. Although the mines did not get everything their own way – they were still heavily taxed for example – many of the uitlander complaints of the pre-war period were attended to by the new government.

The impact of these changes on town and countryside will be explored in the next chapter. The point here is that the South African War and its aftermath marked the end of the protracted process of the conquest of South Africa by settler and imperial powers. African hopes of regaining access to land, encouraged by British rhetoric before and during the war about the injustices of Boer 'Native policy', were dashed. Afrikaner parties won elections held in 1907 for self-governing parliaments in the previous republics (Het Volk in the Transvaal and Orangia Unie in the Free State), and these governments came together with those of Natal and the Cape to form the Union of South Africa in 1910. To the dismay of leading African politicians white supremacy was entrenched in the constitution. Only in the Cape was there a non-racial franchise and even there it is was circumscribed by high property qualifications.

Why, less than ten years after fighting a costly war against the Boers, did the British permit them to dominate the politics of the highveld and the terms of Union? Although Boer troops had been defeated, the outcome of the war was by no means decisive. The terms of the Treaty of Vereeniging had turned the republics into British colonies, but only with promises of internal self-government as

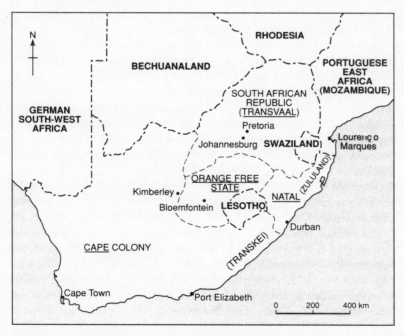

Map 2 The Union of South Africa, 1910 (provinces are underlined) *Source*: adapted from K. Shillington, 1987: *History of Southern Africa*, London: Longman, 137.

31

soon as possible. Once the obstructions of the Kruger government had been removed and the protection of mining interests was assured, the Milner administration aimed at the reconstruction of agriculture to provide food for the urban areas and ensure a profitable and stable local economy. Initial hopes of British immigration on a large scale were not met. Much capital and training in modern farming techniques were instead focused on Boers who were restored to their land. Political unity for the sake of economic growth was thus the British priority. Afrikaner nationalist sentiments needed to be accommodated, provided they could be contained within a single economic and political structure.

Key Boer leaders, such as Smuts, recognized the advantages of this. In place of total independence, a new form of unity could be achieved, provided a measure of Afrikaner political participation was guaranteed. Moreover, British suppression of the Bambatha rebellion (see p. 23) demonstrated the need for white unity in the face of black resistance and showed the Afrikaners that they had little to fear from a political union in which white interests were so clearly upheld.

Economic and political stability required incorporation of Afrikaner politicians into the central organs of government, rather than self-governing Boer provinces. So, contrary to initial expectations, the new constitution of 1910 did not follow the Australian pattern of federalism. Union, with major central government power, was established, albeit with regional concessions in the location of administrative functions; Cape Town was the legislative capital, Pretoria the administrative and Bloemfontein the judicial. In an ominous sign of what lay ahead, white unity was thus upheld at the expense of black political and land rights.

Although at the time it was thought likely that the Union would further expand territorially, in fact the state created in 1910 fixed the boundaries of modern South Africa. The British protectorates of Bechuanaland (later Botswana), Basutoland (Lesotho) and Swaziland were excluded and proposals to incorporate Southern Rhodesia were outvoted in a referendum in that territory in 1922 (Hyam 1972). The only addition of territory came with the invasion of German South West Africa during the First World War and the subsequent mandate granted to South Africa over Namibia by the League of Nations. Namibia was ruled by South Africa until its independence in 1990, although it was never formally part of the country.

The conquest of the land was thus formalized by the Act of Union under a unitary state entrenching white political power. The impact of this process for the lives of its inhabitants is the subject of the remainder of this book.

SUGGESTIONS FOR FURTHER READING

Atmore, A. and Marks, S. 1974: 'The imperial factor in South Africa in the nineteenth century: towards a reassessment'. *Journal of Imperial and Commonwealth History*, 3, 105–39.
Elphick, R. and Giliomee, H. 1989: *The shaping of South African society, 1652–1840*. London and Cape Town: Maskew Miller Longman.
Maylam, P. 1986: *A history of the African people of South Africa: from the Iron Age to the 1970s*. Cape Town: David Philip.

3

Changes in Town and Countryside

As we have seen the discovery of diamonds and gold was central to the colonial conquest of South Africa. The 'Mineral Revolution' also brought about fundamental changes in the economy and society of town and countryside. This chapter will explore some of these changes between the mid-nineteenth century and the 1940s. It was during this period that a capitalist and industrial economic system was introduced into South Africa. This set the scene for the emergence of racial segregation in the late nineteenth and early twentieth centuries and for the policy of apartheid in the late 1940s.

Before the Mineral Revolution

Before the 1870s only some parts of South Africa had been transformed into settler societies. The economy of the mid-nineteenth century Cape colony was dominated by settler commercial agriculture, with private land accumulation, market links and merchant-based credit. This was accompanied by social stratification as some benefited from these trading and capital contacts while others were squeezed out. In the western Cape grain- and wine-producing regions a wealthy market-oriented farmer gentry had emerged by at least the middle of the eighteenth century and settlers were increasingly marginalized into frontier farming (Ross 1986). Until the 1830s these farmers depended primarily on imported slave labour together with some proletarianized Khoi workers. Slave emancipation brought little change to the class structure of the western Cape countryside, however. Lacking access to capital or land, except for subsistence cultivation for a few at mission stations, most freed slaves continued to work as poorly paid wage labourers or labour tenants on settler farms (Worden 1989).

In the rest of the Cape, settler pastoral production was dependent on Khoi and San labour. This was often obtained in exchange for land to graze stock but also by more violent and coercive means such as the capture and indenture of children. But the key transformation took place from the 1830s with the growth of commercial wool production, backed by merchant credit. As a result land values rose, marginal farmers with less access to capital were squeezed out and labour tenants and indigenous subsistence cultivators lost access to land (Kirk 1980; Crais 1986). As Bundy has shown (1986), landlessness created a class of 'poor whites', as well as an indigenous proletariat in the rural society of the Cape at least by the 1860s and probably earlier.

The growth of Cape commercial agriculture was accompanied by an increase in the size, market function and mercantile base of the towns in the colony. Cape Town had acquired banks, a Commercial Exchange and local merchant houses by the 1820s, boosted by British capital (Ross 1989). The network of merchants' activities spread far into the colony. By the 1830s country towns such as Swellendam and Graaff-Reinet were becoming important local commercial centres. After 1850 Port Elizabeth gained ascendancy over Cape Town as the major port and trading centre of the colony, based on the expansion of wool production in the eastern Cape (Mabin 1986).

This commercial capital growth at the Cape also fuelled the trading and later the farming activities of settlers in Natal. However, the use of land and labour in this colony differed markedly from that of the Cape. Profitable commercial farming did not develop until the successful takeoff of sugar farming in the 1870s. Much land was owned by absentee speculators and land companies. Many land-holders found it more profitable to rent to African cultivators than farm commercially on their own account. A conflict of interests arose between rentier landlords and missionaries who supported the maintenance of African peasant production on the one hand, struggling settler farmers competing with indigenous producers and denied access to their labour on the other (Slater 1980).

Before the 1870s sugar planters and other settler farmers depended on credit from the land companies and had little influence on colonial government policy. The government was unwilling to break down

African production and thus lose rent revenues and be faced with the social implications of a landless African proletariat over which it would have to exert control. It therefore provided planters with labour from outside: indentured workers from India and, from the 1870s, migrant workers from the northern and eastern Transvaal and Lourenco Marques (Harries 1987). It was not until the period after the 1870s that greater access to land, labour and capital as well as increased milling technology enabled the growth of large-scale sugar plantations (Richardson 1986). Meanwhile some African cultivators profited by access to local markets. Land-owning Christian missionaries in particular encouraged African involvement in the market economy of Natal. African land purchases took place and cash crop production by kholwa peasant communities flourished in the period between the 1840s and 1880 (Etherington 1985).

African cultivators continued to have access to land and production in many of the trekker polities of the mid-nineteenth-century interior. In the South African Republic many wealthier Boers obtained extensive grants of government land in return for official services to the state, but were unable to farm it directly. Limited markets also limited agricultural commercialization. As in Natal, higher profits could be obtained from rents and taxes on African tenants and 'squatters' than by direct settler farming. The process of land accumulation by the wealthy and powerful meant that some Boers lost out; there were also landless whites working as tenant cultivators in the late-nineteenth-century Transvaal. Where settler conquest of the land had not taken place, local cultivation and social organization continued uninterrupted. However, African farming and social experience in this period was never as isolated and unchanging as is suggested by the stereotype which contrasts it to 'dynamic' settler farming. African polities in South Africa had always responded and adapted to opportunities presented by trade and external market links. This continued to be the case with the expansion of colonial commercial networks. Trade in ivory, skins and cloth, in return for guns, ammunition and other manufactured goods from the Cape ports, Durban and Delagoa Bay, flourished across the sub-continent in the mid-nineteenth century. Moreover migrant workers from societies such as the Pedi and the Tsonga, untouched by colonial conquest, were working on Cape and Natal farms from the 1840s (Delius 1980; Harries 1982). Acquisition of guns or cash and cattle for bridewealth payments gave the stimulus for young men to migrate for temporary periods. At this stage their income was a supplement to local resources rather than the essential source of rural income which migrant labour was to become in the twentieth century.

Members of African societies more closely affected by colonial expansion, such as the Xhosa and Sesotho, were also increasingly involved in the labour market of the Cape by the 1840s. Thus before the 1870s important changes in the lives of many South Africans had been brought about by a colonial merchant-backed credit network, commercial agriculture and accompanying new labour demands. However, African independent cultivation continued unimpeded in many areas outside colonial control and was positively encouraged where settler land claims could not be backed up with landowner production. The region was still a panoply of pre-industrial and largely pre-capitalist societies. The Mineral Revolution was to change this decisively.

The Mineral Revolution

The development of the diamond fields at Kimberley and the gold mines of the Witwatersrand transformed South African society. Not only did they spawn new industrial towns – in the case of Johannesburg, a major city – in the open veld, they also created new demands for labour and agrarian produce which had a major impact on rural societies both nearby and far away from the mines. New classes of industrial workers, capitalist producers and landless farm labourers emerged and competed with the merchants, rentier landlords, artisans, peasants and sharecroppers of the mid-nineteenth century. In short, South Africa acquired a capitalist and industrial economy and society.

Although the growth of the Rand from the late 1880s was the main force behind this transformation, many features of the gold mining industry and the society it produced were prefigured in the diamond fields of Kimberley, particularly the emergence of monopoly company control over production and a racially divided labour force.

Mining activities at Kimberley shifted from individual claims in the initial period of discoveries in the late 1860s and early 1870s to larger-scale amalgamations as small-scale claimholders sold out to more successful or wealthier miners. By the late 1870s and 1880s these in turn were taken over by large-scale joint-stock companies backed by European finance. The need for large amounts of capital to work the deeper-level claims and to drain and shore up earlier diggings meant that individuals or smaller companies were unable to maintain mining activities. This was particularly true when diamond prices fell in the 1870s as increased supply reduced their rarity. By the late 1880s further amalgamations were taking place with large conglomerates dominating the industry, such as de Beers Consolidated Mines under the directorship of Cecil Rhodes. In the 1890s de Beers achieved a virtual monopoly not only over diamond production but also over marketing, a position it maintained after its takeover by Anglo American in the 1920s (Turrell 1987; Worger 1987). This process was supported by the state. Initial support for smallholder claims by the administration of Griqualand West soon gave way to backing of amalgamations. In 1876 a law limiting the size of claims was repealed. After the diamond fields became part of the Cape Colony in 1880 direct backing for the companies took place, symbolized by Rhodes's position as Prime Minister in 1890.

These developments are crucial to an understanding of the racial division of labour which took place on the diamond fields. In the earliest years both blacks and whites joined the rush to them and made claims to diggings. Many employed local labourers; some also sub-contracted claims to shareworkers. By the mid-1870s competition between claimholders and desire by white shareworkers to obtain claims of their own led to increasing demands for control over black claimants and workers. Local merchants also favoured such moves, since they believed that sales of diamonds discovered by African workers were undercutting them. The resulting 'Black Flag Revolt' of 1875 did not stem the tide of shareworker and smallholder dispossession but it did lead to the removal of Southey, the Lieutenant-Governor of Griqualand West who had resisted racial discrimination in digging legislation. After 1876 closer controls over African workers were put into effect by the larger mining companies. Registration passes and fixed contract terms were enforced to limit the ability of labourers to play off one employer against another. In practice these were enforced for black workers rather than white.

In the 1880s the increasingly powerful companies went further. In an attempt to control illicit smuggling of diamonds they attempted to strip search workers leaving the mines. Strikes by white miners followed and the practice was confined to black workers. The most discriminatory device followed from this. Closed compounds were introduced, modelled initially on the compounds used by de Beers for the housing of convict labour. Although prevention of diamond smuggling was the stated reason for compounding, other important advantages to the employers were direct control over workers and the wage savings that could be made by the provision of cheap accommodation and food (Turrell 1984). Initially the compounds were intended for both black and white workers. However, white workers protested strongly and backed their action through the ballot box; in 1886 they outvoted a company candidate in elections and placed a Member of Parliament in power who favoured their interests. They were supported by the small traders and merchants of Kimberley who would lose access to their custom if closed compounding was introduced. As a result, the compounds were implemented for black migrant workers alone.

As Turrell (1987) has shown, it was the power of the large mining companies which made controls such as passes, contracts and closed compounds a possibility. It was also this that led to opposition by white workers and the mobilization of white racism as a means to unite and protect themselves. As a result the Kimberley labour force was racially divided by the 1880s. White workers, increasingly employed in supervisory and skilled positions, lived in the boarding houses and homes of Kimberley, a town almost entirely owned and controlled by de Beers. Black migrant workers lived in the closed compounds where living conditions were initially appalling. It was an unfortunate precedent for South Africa's first industrial town to set.

Similar developments took place on the gold mines of the Rand, although here the scale was much larger and Johannesburg became a more complex urban society than Kimberley. From the digger tents of the 1880s it grew into a city of over a quarter of a million people by 1914, by which time the Rand accounted for 40 per cent of the world's gold production with a capital investment of £125 million (Van Onselen 1982: 1–2).

As on the diamond fields, initial surface-level prospecting on the Rand soon gave way to larger-scale company mining. By the middle of the 1890s exhaustion of accessible deposits near the surface led to the need for deep-level shaft digging, more sophisticated machinery and much greater capital investment. Large conglomerates emerged, backed by Kimberley and European capital, such as Wernher-Beit and Rhodes's Consolidated Gold Fields (Richardson and Van-Helten 1982). As we have seen (pp. 27–8), this required state backing and an infrastructure which the Kruger government seemed unable to provide, resulting in the South African War.

Contrary to twentieth-century belief, South African gold mining was not an inevitable source of great profit. Capital costs were high because of the difficulties of mining the thin gold veins and of the low quality of the ore deposits. Indeed ore of similar quality had been abandoned on the Californian and Australian gold fields as too unprofitable to extract. The gold price was fixed on the world market and although this avoided slumps of the kind which occurred in the diamond price, it also placed a limit on profit levels. In order to recruit the necessary skilled labour, the mine owners had to offer relatively high wages to experienced immigrant miners who were mainly from Britain, Australia and the United States. Thus the only way that they managed to keep up profits was by using particularly cheap unskilled local labour.

According to the early revisionist historians, it was this cost structure that produced the migrant labour system and the colour bar on the mines (see, for example, Johnstone 1976). The gold mines followed the example of Kimberley in using African unskilled migrant workers, housed in compounds, because they could be employed at low wages, sufficient only for the subsistence of single men. The full cost of keeping a family (the cost of reproduction) was met by the rural economies from which workers came and to which they returned (Wolpe 1972). Some recent work has shown that the Rand compounds were not as tightly controlled as those of Kimberley and that a few black mine workers lived in Johannesburg permanently with their families (Moroney 1982). But, as on the diamond fields, pass law controls were used to minimize labour mobility and prevent desertion. They were introduced in 1896, although they were not always rigidly enforced and some mines evaded them and illegally recruited deserters (Levy 1982: 74–80). Another device to reduce wages was to use agents to recruit workers in the rural areas where contracts were signed and terms fixed without giving the worker the opportunity of playing off one employer against another. Monopoly control over labour recruiting developed as large-scale companies came to dominate the industry, but this was not fully achieved until at least the 1920s (Jeeves 1985).

After the South African War, landless whites and ex-soldiers moved from the countryside to the Rand in search of work. The distinction between white immigrant skilled and black migrant unskilled mine labour was thus challenged. But the racial division of labour was maintained because the mine owners could not afford to pay the wages required for the subsistence costs of a fully proletarianized permanent labour force. An experiment of using white unskilled labour at the Village Main Reef Mine failed. Instead the

40

mines continued to use cheaper African migrant labourers or, when these were less readily available in the immediate post-war years, indentured contract workers from China. In 1904 the Labour Ordinance passed by the Transvaal government entrenched the position. This was reinforced after Union by the Mines and Works Act of 1911 which required some jobs to be performed by those holding 'certificates of competency'. In practice the higher-paid skilled positions were restricted to white workers, which implied that unskilled work was to be performed by Africans (Davies 1976). Later attempts by the mine owners to cut costs further by employing cheaper black migrants in skilled jobs led to concerted white labour protest (see pp. 51–2).

Elsewhere in the labour market of the Rand, however, changes were taking place in the early twentieth century. Van Onselen (1982) has shown that before the South African War a number of self-employed Africans found work in Johannesburg outside the mining sector: as domestic workers (especially the Zulu 'houseboys') and washermen serving the needs of the boarding houses of single immigrants, and as brickmakers, builders and transport drivers in the rapidly growing city. By the turn of the century, however, the stabilization of white workers' family housing and the immigration of female white domestic servants reduced the role of independent houseboys and washermen. Electric trams, steam laundries and large-scale building companies drove many self-employed workers out of business. Competition with new Afrikaner migrants from the country-side also increased unemployment. In a bid to win electoral support, the government provided some relief work for unemployed whites but none for the voteless blacks. As a result some unemployed Africans joined the gangs operating around the city, such as the quasi-military 'Regiment of the Hills' under the charismatic leadership of Jan Note. Initially a protest against encroaching proletarianization and unemployment, such gangs survived by robbing both the Johannesburg propertied classes and the migrant workers travelling home with their wages. By the 1910s, such class conflicts were endemic.

At the other end of the social scale, a small African middle class, primarily consisting of teachers, emerged in towns such as Kimberley and Johannesburg. Many had mission education and they provided the leadership of organizations such as the early African National Congress (ANC) (see p. 82).

The complexity of urban society was also increased by the growing numbers of permanent workers in manufacturing industry during the first two decades of the twentieth century. This was especially true of the Rand where engineering works in particular developed alongside the mines. But the impetus of the Mineral Revolution had also spread to other cities. The diamond discoveries restored Cape Town's economic predominance over Port Elizabeth, and Durban became the main port outlet from the Rand. In both places African migrant dock workers were housed in barracks. But the early manufacturing factories which also developed in these cities employed workers who had moved permanently from the rural hinterland. This was the background to much larger-scale urbanization in the 1920s and 1930s.

Increasing numbers of Africans in the towns led to central state intervention. Prior to the 1920s, the housing and administration of Africans was left in the hands of municipal authorities, each of which followed its own policy. In Kimberley and Johannesburg we have seen that many black workers were housed in compounds built by their employers, but others rented accommodation elsewhere in the towns, and in Johannesburg areas of freehold black property ownership, such as Sophiatown, also existed.

Residential segregation originated in towns dominated not by the mining industry but by merchant and commercial interests. In Cape Town bubonic plague in 1901 led to the forced removal of dock workers, who had been the first to be exposed to infection carried in the produce they were unloading, and other African residents from the centre of the town to Ndabeni location on its outskirts. In Port Elizabeth Africans were also expelled during the plague epidemic, although no alternative accommodation was provided and they squatted on land outside the municipal boundaries. Thus the earliest examples of racial segregation were motivated by what has been described as the 'sanitation syndrome' (Swanson 1977). In 1902 legislation enabled Cape municipalities to enforce such measures within their own boundaries, although this was only partially enforced.

In Durban many workers were temporary migrants, taking daily employment and living in the surrounding rural hinterland. Since the late nineteenth century they had been subject to pass controls and obliged to register for employment. Before 1900 racial control over residence in Durban was directed more against Indians than Africans, fuelled by white traders who resented Indian commercial competition in the central areas of the town (Swanson 1983). But as in the Cape, the plague of 1902, together with fears of social upheaval during the 1906 Bambatha uprising, led the Durban and Pietermaritzburg municipalities to enforce segregated residence of Africans in 'native locations'. What was unique to Durban was the system of financing these locations by revenues from municipal monopoly over the brewing of sorghum beer, produced for African consumption. This 'Durban system' solved the problem of how to pay for the building and administration of locations without increasing white rates and taxes (Swanson 1976).

Thus prior to the 1920s a variety of urban segregation measures existed, but they varied from place to place and were only patchily enforced. However, in the period after the First World War greater state intervention took place. Several factors were responsible for this. The 1918 Spanish influenza epidemic, which had a devastating impact on many South African towns, gave rise to renewed 'sanitation syndrome' fears by white residents that infection was spread by black inhabitants. Moreover African political and labour protest on the Rand and elsewhere alarmed the central government and local authorities (see pp. 51–3). Increasing numbers of Africans were migrating permanently to the towns, encouraged by the growth of manufacturing industry, and moving into crowded rented accommodation. This was resented both by white workers who believed wages would be depressed and by traders and property owners who feared competition with the black hawkers and small-scale retailers and saw the value of property declining because of slum developments (Rich 1978).

These pressures led to the establishment of the Stallard Commission whose recommendations were adopted in the Natives (Urban Areas) Act of 1923. This empowered municipalities throughout the country to enforce residential segregation, and it also forbade the further granting of freehold property rights to Africans on the grounds that they were not permanent urban residents and 'should only be permitted within municipal areas in so far and for so long as their presence is demanded by the wants of the white population' (Koch 1983: 153). The Act extended the 'Durban system' throughout the Union by requiring that location costs be defrayed by revenues from African rents and beerhall monopolies.

Alternative proposals made by the government-appointed Godley Committee that Africans with a certain level of education or occupation as traders, artisans or skilled workers should be exempted from such control were rejected. The interests of white workers and traders thus won out over that of manufacturing employers. After the radicalization of the black middle class in Johannesburg, the development of any permanent African presence in the towns was deemed undesirable.

The principles of urban segregation and influx control were thus laid down by the principles of the Stallard Commission. However, the 1923 Act was not uniformly imposed. Municipalities were still free to choose whether they wanted to force Africans into locations, although many responded in the 1920s to pressures to do so from their white voters. Thus in Brakpan, working class whites, resentful of an African presence, demanded segregation and a new location was finally built in 1927 (Sapire 1989b). But areas of black freehold ownership remained, such as Sophiatown and Newclare in Johannesburg. Forced removal could not legally take place unless alternative accommodation had been provided. Many municipalities balked at the costs this would involve with the increasing flow of migrants from the countryside to the towns in the subsequent decades.

Changes in the countryside

The early revisionists argued that migrant labour was used on the mines because it enabled employers to pay low wages. However, more recently some historians have argued that migrant labour was a sign not of the power of a mining economy to control its workers but of the weakness of an economic system that had largely failed to gain control over rural production. Labour migrancy also suited the needs of the workers and the rural societies from which they came, at least in its early phases.

Most migrant workers at Kimberley in the 1870s came from societies which had provided labourers to Cape and Natal farms in the previous decades, particularly the Pedi, Tsonga and Sotho. The Pedi saw the diamond mines as a further source of wages to obtain guns for hunting and defence and to replenish their cattle stock. Delius (1980) suggests that this was under the control and approval of the Pedi chiefs and that land and population pressure meant that increasing local trade and production was not a viable alternative. That they were still in a bargaining position is shown by the fact that in the 1870s they chose to work in Kimberley rather than on the nearby alluvial gold diggings in the Transvaal where wages were lower and guns more expensive.

Kimble (1982) similarly argues that migrants from Basutoland in this period were more in control of the labour market than earlier views suggested. In 1876, for instance, they withdrew their labour from Kimberley and succeeded in obtaining higher wages as a result. Their involvement as workers was also to obtain guns and cash for trading goods, some under the control of the ruling royal lineage and others through Christian converts seeking money to buy private property. Only a few were forced into work by poverty, although after the 1884 annexation of Basutoland and increasing colonial demands for tax payments in cash this became an increasing motivation behind Sotho migrancy.

In the case of the Tsonga, Harries (1982) has shown that decided advantages were to be gained from migrant labour. Young men thereby obtained the means of acquiring cloth, guns and cash for bridewealth, although the chiefs retained close control over labourers and recruiters and there was increased exploitation of women who bore the brunt of local production while men were away. Again the bargaining power of Tsonga workers was demonstrated in 1890–1 when they abandoned the Rand after mine owners attempted to lower wages.

In the early years of the Mineral Revolution therefore, only some African societies provided migrant workers and they did so largely on their own terms. Others had no need or desire to be involved in mine labour. For instance, the Thlaping, who inhabited the region around Kimberley, provided very few workers for the mines until the 1880s. Higher returns were obtainable from crop production for the rapidly growing market of the town, although the development of commercial farming did bring increasing disparity of wealth and some poorer Thlaping did then migrate to the mines (Shillington 1982). Similarly few Zulu workers came to the diamond mines in the earlier years. Local production and trade in Zululand was uninterrupted and chiefly control over surplus gave individuals no incentive or means for wage labour (Guy 1982).

From the 1880s, however, this situation changed markedly. As we have seen (pp. 19–21), the difficulty of getting labour was a major factor behind the intensification of colonial conquest and land control during this period. Colonial administrators imposed new taxes on African subjects, such as the hut tax assessed per household, which had to be paid in cash. Unlike earlier tributes to chiefs which had been in kind, colonial taxes did not lessen in times of harvest failure, drought or cattle disease. Thus hut taxes imposed on the Thlaping in 1877 and extended after the 1878 rebellion forced labourers into dependence on cash wages, and Tswana migrants appeared on the mines in the 1880s. Likewise the reconstruction of Zulu society after colonial conquest replaced military service and tribute to chiefs with hut taxation and cash demands. From 1888 Zulu migrants became an increasingly important source of Rand labour. The need to ensure that migrant wages returned to Natal led its government to support the migrancy system developed in the Transvaal and Cape. Local colonial authorities thus replaced African chiefs in their drive to control mine wages.

Rinderpest and drought ensured the continued flow of migrant workers in the 1890s. However, the disruption of mine production during the South African War and the recovery by Africans of some land and cattle in its aftermath meant that migrant supplies fell in the 'reconstruction' period. Africans were thus still able to resist full dependence on wage earnings, and this factor led to the introduction of Chinese indentured labourers. Only with further state intervention after Union and natural disasters such as drought and East Coast fever in 1911–12 were adequate African migrant labour supplies again forthcoming. Moreover by the 1910s, African migrant workers were also being used more extensively on white-owned farms in areas such as East Griqualand, the eastern Transvaal and Natal. On the Natal sugar plantations they increasingly came to supplement the work force after the ending of Indian indentured labour in 1911.

Migrant labour was not the only response of African societies to the Mineral Revolution. We have seen that one of the means of resisting wage labour was to cultivate crops for commercial production, thus raising the required cash for trading goods and colonial taxes. Bundy (1972, 1979) has shown that in the late nineteenth century many African cultivators became peasant farmers, producing a surplus which was sold to the growing markets of the towns and which was given a particular impetus by the rise of the mineral centres. There were wide regional variations in this response depending on market links and access to land. In the Ciskei, Transkei and Basutoland a prosperous peasant class emerged between the 1830s and the 1880s, particularly amongst people such as the Mfengu who had control over land, and centres such as Queenstown became key grain markets for the region. Stratification also took place. Some peasant producers hired labour and expanded their land holdings while others lost the means of subsistence and became labourers for African or colonial cultivators.

In Natal the kholwa mission-based peasantry similarly benefited from the increasing market for produce from the 1870s and by the 1880s they were purchasing land in northern Natal. By then other

African cultivators and tenants were producing for an external market, including some who turned to sugar production.

In the Transvaal and Orange Free State republics African land ownership had been restricted by trekker legislation, but many black tenants on Boer land nonetheless benefited from the expanded market of the late nineteenth century and became prosperous producers. Some paid cash rents to absentee landlords (either individuals or land companies) while others worked for a part of the year for the land owner in return for occupation of their own plots, a system known as labour tenancy. In the Free State in particular, sharecropping arrangements existed by which the tenant gave over a proportion (usually half) of his crop in return for use of the land. This gave less capitalized landlords access to crops which they did not themselves produce. It also enabled sharecroppers to profit from selling their part of the produce to traders (Keegan 1982).

Some more recent writers have questioned aspects of Bundy's argument about the emergence of an African peasantry. The precise interaction between precolonial social formations and the development of a new peasant class needs closer attention. Emphasis on market production also fails to highlight the actual organization of production and the extent to which producers were independent of other forces. For instance Beinart (1982) has shown that in Pondoland (part of the Transkei) in the early twentieth century both peasant production and migrant labour expanded together. Cattle advances made by labour recruiters to household heads enabled local production to expand and it was not until the 1930s that the decline of market production led to total dependence on migrant wages.

What is clear, however, is that the prosperity of African peasants did not last. Sharecropping benefited white rentier landlords who lacked the capital to employ wage labourers, but the growth of a vibrant African class of market-oriented cultivators did not find favour with many settler farmers. In many parts of the Rand's rural hinterland on the highveld, some white farmers were actively participating in commercial production at the expense of poorer whites and in competition with market-oriented African peasants (Trapido 1986, Morrell 1986). Colonial governments also had little access to peasant profits, and by the end of the century the mining companies realized that peasant cultivation was holding much of the labour in the countryside that they required in the towns. A barrage of legislation followed, restricting and ultimately destroying peasant production.

In the eastern Cape the Glen Grey Act, passed by the Rhodes administration in 1894, limited the amount of land each family could own, thus restricting wealthy African producers, and also taxed non wage-earners. It was only applied in limited areas initially, but similar controls were extended to other parts of the Cape by 1910. Laws against squatting, or the occupation of land by cultivators who did not own it, and controls over surplus production by tenants were also more rigidly enforced in the early 1900s.

In Natal the increasing viability of white commercial farming by the 1890s and the control of settlers over the state after the granting of responsible government in 1893 led to pressure on African producers. The land companies and the government sold farms to settlers and evicted many squatters living on them, while rising land values led to increased rents for those who were permitted to stay. Purchase of land by Africans in Natal was forbidden in 1903 (Slater 1975).

In the Transvaal legislation against squatting had existed since 1887. However, it was only patchily enforced. During the South African War the destruction of many Boer farms meant that African-produced food supplies were needed on the Rand. But Het Volk's victory in the 1907 Transvaal elections (see p. 31) was largely based on its promise to restore white rural hegemony at the expense of African producers. The squatting laws were more rigidly enforced, largely in the interests of white farmers (Trapido 1978).

In the Free State African land ownership had long been effectively forbidden. However, the government intervened after 1907 to promote settler agriculture at the expense of African tenants and sharecroppers. As Keegan (1986) has shown, opposition to African peasant production on the southern highveld was accentuated by the growing impoverishment after the 1870s of many white tenants (bywoners) and sharecroppers. It was not only African farmers who were squeezed out by the stratification of wealth which followed commercial farming. There were also 'poor whites' on the highveld, who had no access to land and who increasingly migrated to the towns or competed on the land with African tenants. In this they were often at a disadvantage because of their unwillingness to make use of family labour. Thus although absentee landlords and less-capitalized land-owners benefited from African tenant and cropper production, by 1907 poor-white populism joined white commercial farmers in opposing black peasant cultivation. Increasingly strident attacks were made on black cultivators, often marked by violence against them and the landowners who rented to them.

It was in this context that the Union government passed the Natives Land Act of 1913. The Act forbade the purchase or lease of land by Africans outside designated areas known as reserves. These were far removed from white-owned farms and the key areas of commercial agriculture. It thus extended the ban on African land ownership in the Free State to the majority of the Union. In addition, sharecropping was forbidden in the Free State where its existence had caused heightened poor white opposition, and labour tenants were required to provide at least ninety days of work for their landlords.

The long-term significance of the Act was enormous. It removed the means by which many African producers had resisted both incorporation into the migrant labour system of the mines and wage labour on the farms. For this reason it has been described as the product of the alliance of 'gold and maize' which the Act of Union brought to political power (Trapido 1970). Moreover it established the principle of land segregation and defined the boundaries of the 'Native Reserves'. Initially covering only 7 per cent of the land area of

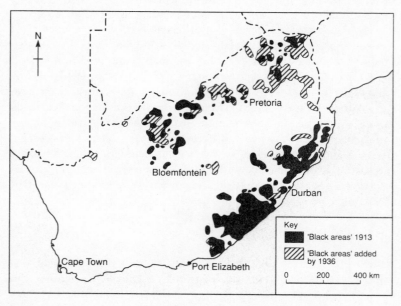

Map 3 'Native reserves', 1913 and 1936 *Source*: adapted from D. Denoon and B. Nyeko, 1984: *Southern Africa since 1800*, 2nd edn, London: Longman, 168.

the Union, increased to 14 per cent in 1936, these areas became the basis of the 'homelands' of the apartheid era.

The immediate effect of the 1913 Act has been debated by historians. It certainly gave white farmers, particularly those in the Free State, the power to evict croppers and other tenants who would not submit to full control of their time and labour by the landowner. It thus acted as a catalyst to the changes already taking place on the land with the extension of white commercial farming, using wage or labour tenancy. Africans had little opportunity to own land in the majority of the country although many continued to work it as tenants. Sol Plaatje, the secretary of the newly formed South African Native National Congress (later renamed the African National Congress), described vividly in his *Native Life in South Africa* his experiences on the highveld where he 'met many a native family with their stock, turned out by the Act upon the roads' (1916).

There is no doubt that immense disruption and suffering followed the passing of the Land Act. It was not, however, immediately enforceable throughout the Union. In 1917 it was declared illegal in the Cape because the Act of Union had preserved the African voting rights in that province, which depended on land ownership. And even outside the Cape, as Keegan (1986) has shown, the legislative ideal was proving unattainable. Relatively few white landowners were able to afford to convert to wage labour, and many continued to rent land to African tenants or sharecroppers well into the 1940s. Many croppers left the Free State but settled on farms elsewhere, particularly in the southern Transvaal. In the areas demarcated as 'reserves', the Land Act promoted African land purchase.

The Land Act thus had a differential impact depending on local circumstances. Nonetheless it was a clear marker of the increasing pressures that had been exerted on black landowners and commercial producers and of the dramatic changes in the countryside that accompanied the mineral revolution.

Conflict in town and countryside

By 1914 the balance of power in both town and countryside was shifting in favour of the capitalist and capitalizing sectors of the economy. The subsequent years were marked by continuing struggles of urban and rural workers as they sought to resist the full impact of proletarianization: struggles of ordinary men and women that have for long gone unnoticed in the general history of South Africa.

On the Rand disputes centred around the conflicts between the mine owners and mine workers, but were complicated by the racial divisions of interest within the labour force. White workers fought to maintain their position against attempts by mining companies to replace them with cheaper black migrant workers. By the early twentieth century, African workers had certainly acquired the expertise for work such as rock drilling, which had originally been performed by immigrant miners. Mine owners moved to employ them at lower wages than their white predecessors, but maintained the racial skilled–unskilled division by declaring such work 'deskilled'. White miners were increasingly being used only for supervisory positions and in fewer numbers.

White miners fought back to retain their privileged position. In 1907 a strike was defeated by the use of Afrikaner scab labourers, but in 1913 a major strike against deskilling was combined with demands for trade union recognition: a common cause of labour disputes throughout the world at the time, but one which in South Africa took on a racially exclusive overtone. This achieved some success, and in the following year a general strike of white workers, beginning in the railways and extending to the mines, protested against the increased use of black labour: white skilled and unskilled workers were by then drawing together in racially exclusive causes. This protest also led to increasing support for the South African Labour Party, led by F.S. Cresswell who had unsuccessfully attempted to run a mine using only white labour. In 1914, Labour won the highest number of seats in the Transvaal Provincial administration, which considerably alarmed the mine owners. After the disruption of the First World War, the Status Quo Act in 1918 defused such militancy by fixing the job colour bar on the mines, representing a victory for white workers (Davies 1979).

This period was also marked by black worker militancy, at least in part inspired by the tangible benefits obtained by white worker action. Between 1915 and 1917 there was protest in some of the compounds against living conditions and high prices in the mine stores, exacerbated by inflation and increasing impoverishment in the reserves which led to greater demands on migrants' earnings. In addition protest amongst permanently urbanized African workers on the Rand was growing. Johannesburg sanitary workers struck for higher wages in 1918 but also in protest against pass law regulations and inadequate housing. The speed with which the municipality gave in to white worker demands at this period furthered African militancy. Supported by an increasingly radical Transvaal Native Congress, calls for increased pay and passive resistance to pass controls spread amongst the municipal workers (Bonner 1982). Frustration on the mines was increased by the Status Quo Act and the ability of unskilled Afrikaner workers coming from the countryside to obtain higher-paid 'skilled' jobs, while experienced African workers found their positions steadily downgraded in status. A major strike of African mine workers broke out in 1920, which although suppressed did lead to some easing of the job colour bar as employers sought to co-opt radicalized skilled workers.

The division of interest between black and white mine workers was by now deeply entrenched. Any concession to one group threatened the position of the other. The increased militancy of the 1920 strike, and the concessions made in its wake, made white workers fear that they would lose the ground gained after 1913. In the slump of 1919–20, mine owners attempted to reduce white wages again. Negotiations between the trade unions and employers broke down during 1921, and some of the whites employed in semi-skilled positions guaranteed by the Status Quo Act were replaced by cheaper African migrant workers. Refusal of the mine owners to negotiate further led to growing trade union militancy, fuelled by examples of worker resistance in Russia and Germany. The result was a general strike of white workers and the insurrection of the 1922 'Rand Revolt'.

Backed by the newly formed Communist Party of South Africa, workers elected strike committees and formed strike commandos. The red flag flew over Johannesburg Town Hall and alongside union banners in marches and demonstrations in the city. Afrikaner and English-speaking workers were united in action. But the strikers were not only mobilized on class lines. They were also virulently opposed to black workers whom they saw as competitors. Attacks were made on compounds and on African working-class areas. One slogan paraded at striker meetings vividly displayed the combination of white racism and the influence of the international labour movement: 'Workers of the world unite and fight for a White South Africa.'

The Rand Revolt was suppressed with the armed power of the government which demonstrated its support for the employers in no uncertain terms. Prime Minister Jan Smuts ordered in army troops and planes and bombed the white working-class suburbs of Benoni and Germiston. Over 200 strikers were killed. As a result the strike was broken, white wages fell and some blacks were employed in their place. However, the events of 1922 led to the implacable opposition of white workers to the Smuts government, which was voted out of office two years later. The new 'Pact' government combined worker support for the Labour Party and Afrikaner nationalists from rural areas. It marked a new drive towards racial segregation, as we shall see in the next chapter.

The increased radicalism of workers on the Rand in the post-First World War period was paralleled by labour conflicts elsewhere in urban South Africa. Although the Native Congress in Johannesburg had come to see the need to support worker interests, elsewhere the impetus was taken up by unofficial black labour unions. In Cape Town a strike by dock workers in 1919 for better pay and conditions led to the formation of a union under the leadership of Clements Kadalie. Although the strike was a failure, it demonstrated the possibility of organized labour, and in the following few years the union extended its membership elsewhere in South Africa. Wage protests had also taken place in Bloemfontein, where another union was formed under Selby Msimang, and some organized protest also took place in the docks at East London and Port Elizabeth. In 1920 representatives of these worker organizations, together with others from Kimberley and the Rand, met together in Bloemfontein with the aim of forming 'one great union of skilled and unskilled workers of South Africa, south of the Zambezi' (Wickins 1978: 61).

The Industrial and Commercial Workers' Union (ICU) thus formed obtained much more support than black political organiz-ations such as the ANC during the 1920s, boasting a membership of over 100,000 at its height. It presented the alarming spectre to employers of organized protest by a new black working class. Furthermore it derived support from the black lower middle classes who were losing out in an increasingly segregated society. Many of the leaders of the ICU were mission educated or were skilled artisans who were finding common cause with the demands and grievances of workers (Bradford 1984). However, the ICU impact on urban workers declined after its early impetus. Internal struggles emerged between members of the Communist Party who joined the ICU after orientating themselves towards black, rather than white, worker interests, and Kadalie and other early leaders. Other regional divisions and disputes left the ICU weakened in the face of state and employer opposition, and it was a spent force by the end of the 1920s.

However, the ICU ultimately obtained most of its support from the countryside. Rural protest in the 1920s was widespread, reflecting the dislocations and class tensions which the agrarian changes of the past few decades had produced. This was a different kind of resistance

53

from that made by Africans to colonial conquest which we examined in the last chapter. It was rather the response to the increasing intervention of the colonial state in the reserves and growing pressure on tenants of white-owned land.

Such conflicts had been evident from the 1890s. In a series of studies of the reserve territories of the Transkei and eastern Cape, Beinart and Bundy (1987) have identified changing forms of resistance as the region moved from one of a predominantly peasant or subsistence rural economy to one of dependence on migrant labour and active state intervention and control. In the East Griqualand region in the 1890s there was opposition to hut taxes, landlord rents and labour demands from nearby settler farmers, and headmen responded in a variety of ways ranging from collaboration to open defiance of the colonial state.

After the South African War a further range of forms of resistance to colonial taxes and land controls (such as the extension of the Glen Grey Act) took place: delegations to government officials and petitions, passive resistance such as refusal to pay taxes or to register land tenancies and overt resistance to government measures such as cattle-dipping or compulsory movement of livestock. Between 1908 and 1916 dipping tanks were destroyed, fees withheld, telegraph lines cut and trading stores – symbols of penetration of colonial merchants – burnt down. In the Herschel district of the eastern Cape, rising prices and inflation in the period after the First World War led to boycotts of trading stores, often organized by women cultivators. By the mid-1920s similar actions for similar reasons were taken against schools, land registration officials and other symbols of external intervention into local society. Action was also increasingly taken against local headmen and chiefs who were seen to be collaborating with the colonial authorities.

Another sign of social dislocation and rejection of the colonial presence in the reserves was the growth of independent churches. Many groups of African Christians broke away from the established churches and missions in the late nineteenth and early twentieth centuries and formed 'Ethiopian' churches identifying with African Christian roots.

In some cases, such separatist religious movements acquired strong millenarian overtones and rejected earthly authorities in a way which alarmed the government. For instance, in 1921, in an action which prefigured his suppression of the Rand Revolt, Smuts ordered the forced removal of the Israelites, a group of independent African

Christians led by the prophet Enoch Mgijima, from the village they had occupied at Bulhoek near Queenstown, on the grounds that they were 'illegal squatters', refusing access to local officials and fomenting rebellion. At least 183 people were killed and 129 wounded in the process. The Israelites gained support because, in the years after the First World War, African producers experienced impoverishment of the reserve economy, inflation and increased taxation. Resistance was also encouraged by news of the Rand strike in 1920 (Edgar 1982).

The links between protests in the towns and in the reserves were also revealed by the 'Wellington movement', which attracted considerable support in the Transkei in the late 1920s. Its leader, Wellington Butelezi, had been much influenced by ideas stemming from Marcus Garvey's United Negro Improvement Association (UNIA) in the United States which rejected integration into white society and called for 'Africa for the Africans'. Branches of the UNIA had been set up in South African cities such as Cape Town and Durban. In the Wellington movement Garveyite ideas combined with rural Ethiopianism to produce a 'rural Africanism' (Beinart and Bundy 1987: 341) which brought together both traditional rural leaders and ideologies and the support of those who had obtained missionary and colonial education but were marginalized by the growing segregation of the period. It had formal links with the Cape Town branch of the UNIA but acquired a millenarian overtone, linking with rural Ethiopianism, in its belief that American 'Negroes' would come and liberate black South Africans from their white oppressors. Although millenarian expectations were not realized, support for Garveyism in the rural Transkei continued well into the 1930s (Hill and Pirio 1987).

Although study of other regions is still needed, it is clear enough from these examples of the eastern Cape and Transkei that African resistance in a variety of forms characterized the rural areas in the decades after colonial conquest. They also provide a necessary background to the spread of the influence of the ICU from the towns into the countryside that took place in the late 1920s.

Bradford (1987) has shown how the ICU changed its focus from the urban-based movement of the early 1920s to a predominantly rural organization by 1927, with support from both the reserves and workers and labour tenants on the white-owned farms, especially in the eastern Cape, the Natal Midlands, Pondoland, parts of the Free State and the eastern Transvaal. This was a period of increasing pressure on rural labourers. Land hunger, aggravated by the Land

Act, was widespread in the reserves, particularly in Natal. On white-owned farms a worldwide agricultural depression led to lowering of produce prices and many farmers found themselves in debt. Often they attempted to pass on the burden of such difficulties by lowering amounts paid to wage labourers or by increasing the labour or sharecropping demands and rents of their tenants. As a result the late 1920s saw a marked increase in the number of Africans drawn into urban labour and a tendency for more women and children to work in the fields. In those areas where farmers could benefit from using land for commercial crop cultivation, such as on the highveld maize belt and the Natal wattle plantations, tenant farmers were evicted.

The ICU attracted widespread support in this situation. It identified land dispossession, rent increases and low wages as key issues for which to struggle, and associated particular local grievances with national campaigns for action against the monopoly of white land ownership. In differing regions the emphasis of protest varied according to the character of local social relations. In the western and southern Cape, fully proletarianized farm workers demanded higher wages. In parts of Natal, the Transvaal and the Free State, the dominant issues were land access for tenant farming and opposition to mechanization and to increased rent and labour demands. In many reserves state intervention in the form of taxation and authoritarian control by government-appointed chiefs provided the main fuel of protest.

The ICU thus gave legitimacy to a wide range of local needs. Its campaigns became increasingly radical, from deputations and appeals in court to passive resistance against removals and pass laws, cattle maiming and organized farm labour strikes. Inevitably it encountered implacable opposition both from landowners and from the state. Throughout the country, but particularly in Natal, meetings were broken up, ICU organizers were lynched and members were dismissed or lost their tenancy leases. Although the ICU did successfully challenge illegal evictions in the courts, this was an expensive procedure. There was little that could be done to protect workers and tenants from wage losses, and the law in general upheld the interests and property of white farmers.

The lack of tangible benefits gradually lost the ICU support. Its radical policies also lessened. By 1929, Transvaal ICU officials agreed with commercial farmers that the tenant system was undesirable. The failure of the ICU to meet the expectations of its members was accompanied by accusations that organizers were appropriating funds for their own use. By the end of the 1920s the organization had collapsed. It had given a sense of unity to diverse local struggles and had briefly combined urban and rural issues into a national movement where 'a taste of freedom' could be felt. It had achieved an unprecedented level of support throughout the Union and its memory was maintained for many decades afterwards, but nothing more tangible had been achieved.

The national political organizations largely failed to identify with the kinds of struggles and grievances being faced by the majority of South Africans. There were some exceptions: a radicalized branch of the ANC in the western Cape supported calls for higher wages and better working conditions by farm workers in 1929–30, but it found little support from the organization's national leadership with whom it eventually split. The Communist Party adopted a policy calling for agrarian change in 1928 but it was comparatively unsuccessful in attracting rural support and its brief flirtation with the ICU came to grief. It was not until the late 1940s that organized political support for rural struggles re-emerged, particularly in the Transkei (Bundy 1987a).

The conflicts of the 1910s and 1920s demonstrated resistance to new forms of state and employer control over many South Africans in both town and countryside who were caught up in the uneven transition to a capitalist economy and society. Most were unable to reverse the process of economic change, although white workers did achieve gains at the expense of their black counterparts and these were cemented in policies of the government in the 1920s. African protest was less successful, and lacked the link with political mobilization. This was not to come for several decades, as we shall see in the next chapter.

The Depression and its aftermath: the 1930s and 1940s

We have seen that many important changes had taken place in town and countryside by the 1920s, particularly the growth of industry and an urban workforce and the strengthening of commercial agriculture at the expense of black peasants and sharecroppers and white bywoners. Yet these processes were still very incomplete. By the end of the 1940s they were much further advanced, with the growth of manufacturing industry alongside the mining economy, increasing

57

pressure on farm tenants and the impoverishment of the reserves with the consequent marked inflow of rural inhabitants to the towns.

Part of the reason for this was political. Davies et al. (1976) have argued that the Pact government of the National Party and the Labour Party which came to power in 1924 represented primarily white commercial farmers and local manufacturers, breaking the monopoly of mine owner interests which Smuts's previous government had upheld. They argue that this hegemony of 'national' capital (as opposed to 'imperial' mining capital) continued during the Fusion government which brought Smuts back into power in coalition with Hertzog's National Party in 1933. This argument may over-emphasize the significance of change in 1924 since much was done before then to encourage commercial farming and local industry and the mines still dominated the economy in the 1930s. Nonetheless it is true that state intervention was crucial to the social and economic changes of the inter-war years.

The event of greatest significance during this period stemmed from outside South Africa. The Great Depression of the early 1930s marked a turning point. The value of exports, including diamonds, fell. Commercial farmers and local industries were badly hit by falling prices. However, once the fixed gold price was abandoned by Britain and South Africa in 1933, its rapid increase provided a major source of revenue to the Union and a major stimulus for industrial growth.

The support of the state for white farmers was most marked in this period of crisis. Between 1930 and 1932 control boards were established to keep prices above international levels and thus protect local producers of dairy produce, wheat, maize and meat. Protective tariffs against imports of such items as sugar were increased. Although these were initially intended as temporary measures to deal with the problems of the Depression, the principle of state subsidization of commercial farmers was extended in the face of industrial competition. Thus in 1937 the Marketing Act established price controls for rural produce, artificially keeping rural incomes at a level commensurate with those of urban manufacturers (Wilson 1971: 140).

These measures favoured large landowners marketing their own produce. But the impoverishment of small-scale cultivators and tenants, so clearly under way in the earlier part of the century, continued apace. In addition to the problems caused by the Depression, droughts between 1930 and 1933 depleted livestock. The partisan interest of the government was also revealed in its

58

response to such poverty. 'Poor whites', always present, now became acutely visible. Many were bywoners, finally driven from the land by depression and drought and unable to find work in the towns. Their cause was taken up by the Dutch Reformed Church and by the National Party which had its eye on potential voters, and was highlighted by the findings of the Carnegie Commission in 1932 that over 20 per cent of adult Afrikaner males were indigent. State-subsidized relief schemes and job creation programmes were introduced, the most significant of which was the founding of the state-owned iron and steel corporation, ISCOR. Other government-controlled sectors, such as the railways, fired black workers and replaced them with whites. Such policies were not altogether new. Relief schemes for poor whites were provided on the Rand in the 1910s. But the national scale of the schemes in the 1930s was more akin to those carried out by other countries affected by the Depression, such as the United States and Germany. The difference was that in South Africa aid to the poor and unemployed was racially exclusive (Wilson and Ramphele 1989: 318).

No such support was provided by the state for blacks in the reserves or for the labour tenants on white-owned farms. Impoverishment in many parts of the reserves was steadily growing. Although some areas, such as parts of the Transkei, remained reasonably self-sufficient in food production until the 1950s, elsewhere the poverty was acute. Many people were landless, particularly in the Ciskei and the northern Transvaal, and the Native Affairs Commission of 1930–2 noted that some heavily populated regions were fast becoming 'desert areas'. Most households were dependent on wages from migrants to the towns or white farms. Unemployment during the Depression cut off such income while those who could obtain work were willing to do so for very low wages. To this extent, part of the original aim of the mining industry to obtain cheap labour had succeeded. But the impoverishment of the reserves meant that subsistence production for the migrant's family was no longer guaranteed. Pressure for Africans to move permanently to the towns was growing.

Various attempts were made in the late 1930s and 1940s to deal with the crisis in the reserves. The Native Affairs Department identified overstocking and land erosion as the main problems, but attempted to resolve them by stock culling and improvement schemes which took little account of levels of human poverty and encountered fierce opposition (Moll 1988).

The only alternative was to grant more land for reserve cultivation. This was a major political issue in the early 1930s, demanded by organizations such as the ANC and ultimately recognized by the government. As early as 1916, the Beaumont Commission had recommended increasing the size of the reserves. But nothing was done until 1936 with the passing of the Native Trust and Land Act. This provided for the addition of land to the reserves established by the 1913 Land Act, although they still only covered 14 per cent of the country and since some of this was land that Africans still held in freehold it did little to relieve population pressure. Moreover, government funds were set up to enable purchase of reserve land by chiefs for communal distribution, thus limiting individual ownership and the possibility of commercial farming. The Cape, exempted from the 1913 Act, was now brought into line with the rest of the Union, since its limited African franchise was abolished (see p. 75).

The 1936 Act also affected black tenants on white-owned land. The Pact government had consistently supported the demands of white farmers for a cheap labour force and control over independent tenant 'squatters' (Lacey 1981: 120–80). In 1926 the Master and Servant Amendment Act gave farmers extended legal powers over their tenants. In 1932, at the height of the Depression, the Native Service Contract Act forced all tenants on white-owned farms either to work between three and six months per year for the landowner or to pay a heavy £5 tax, and it also prevented them from leaving the farm without written permission. In 1936 this policy was furthered. Farmers were fined who employed sharecroppers or squatters that did not work as labour tenants, and in the Transvaal and Natal the minimum period of labour service was six months.

These clauses were not immediately enforceable, any more than those of the 1913 Land Act had been. But the assault on independent production for black 'squatter' tenants and sharecroppers was certainly now intensified. The trend towards full-time wage labour for blacks on 'white land' was greatly accentuated. Meanwhile state subsidies and mechanization encouraged commercial farming for whites. The agrarian economy outside the reserves was thus well on the way to being fully capitalized, although historians argue about just how complete that process was before the 1950s.

For most blacks the alternative to low-paid farm work or impoverishment in the reserves was to seek work in the towns. This was not easy. During the Depression job opportunities shrank and pass controls also stemmed permanent black urbanization. For instance, the strict rural measures embodied in the 1936 Native Trust and Land Act were followed in the following year by an intensification of urban pass laws in the Native Laws Amendment Act.

However, the situation eased after the end of the Depression and particularly with the abandonment of the gold standard and the impetus this gave to manufacturing industry. Some secondary industry had flourished in the 1920s, particularly engineering works servicing the mines and also clothing manufacture. But during the 1930s it expanded markedly. Industrial growth was evident both on the Rand, where the towns of the East Rand flourished, and in the port cities of Cape Town, Durban, Port Elizabeth and East London. During the Second World War manufacturing industry was given a further major boost, and to meet the labour demands of the factories the pass laws were suspended entirely in 1942–3.

This 'Second Industrial Revolution' was accompanied by something of a 'Second Great Trek'. The rural poor, both black and white, flocked to the towns. In the earlier phase of this process many such workers were Afrikaners, particularly women in the garment industry of the Rand and the Cape. However, by the mid-1930s factories were also employing many black workers, both men and women, not only because they were prepared to accept low wages, but also because by then white workers were in short supply (Freund 1989: 102–3). The number of Africans living in the towns increased markedly during these years, approximately doubling between 1921 and 1936 and increasing again by two-thirds between 1936 and 1948 (Maylam 1986: 179).

Most of the newcomers had come to stay. Whole families, single women and youths came to the towns, driven by the poverty of the countryside and the hope of some form of income in the cities. Some married women from the reserves and Basutoland ran away from the patriarchal control of their husbands and rural chiefs and eked out an existence on their own in the anonymity of the Rand (Bonner 1990a). By the 1940s the majority of the black urban population were no longer migrants but permanent residents who had broken economic ties with the rural areas.

Lack of sufficient housing was a major problem. Few towns had provided any special accommodation for African newcomers, and even those that did, such as Cape Town which built the 'model' Langa township in 1927, found that they were woefully inadequate by the 1940s. The bachelor compounds and hostels of the Rand or Durban could not meet the needs of whole families. As a result many newcomers rented rooms, or backyard spaces, in the crowded slums of the city centres, such as District Six in Cape Town or Doornfontein in Johannesburg, or from African freeholders in the few places where they existed, such as Sophiatown. Poverty and over-crowding were endemic. One contemporary study of 'Rooiyard' in Doornfontein reported that 235 adults and 141 children lived in a confined space of 107 tiny rooms, built back to back with no ventilation or sanitation (Hellman 1935).

Many of these backyard areas were condemned by the Slums Act of 1934 and 'cleared'. In Johannesburg residents were moved to the new township set up at Orlando in 1936, but this was far from the city centre and still inadequate for local needs. Many newcomers were thus forced to squat illegally. By the mid-1940s large shanty settlements had grown up around the Rand, on the Cape Flats and at Hout Bay near Cape Town, at Cato Manor in Durban and on many other plots of otherwise unoccupied land around the towns. They were the product of continued family migration, low wages, unem-ployment and high rents in the landlord-owned properties and municipal locations.

Not all urban dwellers succeeded in finding regular wage employ-ment. Instead many eked out an existence in the 'informal sector' as hawkers, small-scale traders or herbalists. Women who were unable to find employment as domestic servants often took in washing or, more profitably, brewed beer for sale in home-based shebeens (Hellman 1935). Many municipalities placed controls over such activities, demanding licences and fixed stands as a means of limiting competition with white traders and of raising revenue. Shebeens were usually illegal, since municipalities set up their own beerhalls and wanted to monopolize liquor sales. This 'Durban system' of financing township administration (see p. 43) was recommended in the 1923 Natives (Urban Areas) Act and was widely used on the Rand in the late 1930s (La Hausse 1988: 22–8). Police raids against shebeens were thus a constant hazard.

This environment produced a distinctive popular culture known as 'marabi'. This was centred on the shebeens of the Rand and the Pretoria location at Marabastad in the mid-1930s. It was marked by distinctive music, influenced by ragtime and jazz but also incorporat-ing a variety of rural and missionary-influenced styles in a new urban genre (Coplan 1985: 90–112). But marabi was more than entertain-ment. It represented a distinctive way of life, impenetrable to outsiders, which helped to deal with poverty and the 'lack of visible means of subsistence' (Koch 1983). Collective assistance, such as the *stokvel* by which meagre funds were pooled between households, voluntary associations and burial societies provided both the means of economic survival in harsh circumstances and a sense of local identity which at least partially overrode diverse rural backgrounds. Parallels to these features of marabi developed elsewhere. For instance in Cape Town's District Six in the 1930s and 1940s popular music, carnival and self-help organizations provided the basis of a distinctive slum culture (Nasson 1989).

Marabi was also a strongly working-class culture which provided the means of resisting the dominant ethos of both the white and the black middle class in urban society. It was weakened by the clearing of the slumyards in the late 1930s, and was also threatened by the intervention of liberal outsiders who established new organizations and sports clubs in an attempt to 'tame' an alien and potentially threatening urban sub-culture. It nonetheless provided the basis of the distinctive township culture of the succeeding decades.

Marabi may have been a form of cultural resistance, but the cities were also the focus of more overt conflicts in the inter-war years. In the late 1920s and early 1930s a series of attacks on municipal beerhalls took place in Durban and on the Rand. They were largely carried out by women whose home-brewing activities were threatened by such institutions, which also represented municipal authority and control, but they were also at least partially inspired by the collective resistance of town and countryside represented by the ICU. In the 1930s disillusionment with mass organization and the stringencies of the Depression years produced a decade of relative calm. In the 1940s, however, urban protest emerged in more overtly politicized forms reflecting the needs of its more fully proletarianized participants.

Increased living costs in the early 1940s led to a number of community-based actions. Rent boycotts and stayaways took place on the Rand and elsewhere. In 1944 there was a stayaway in Brakpan sparked by the dismissal of a local ANC teacher but reflecting wider discontent with rent levels, living conditions and wages (Sapire 1987). A series of bus boycotts in the Alexandra township near Johannesburg between 1940 and 1945 forced the municipality to subsidize fares. The greater bargaining power of urban blacks in the war period undoubtedly led to some victories, although calls for general opposition to segregation were less successful than campaigns around immediate local issues (Stadler 1981).

Johannesburg squatters also took collective action in the war years. Opposition to attempts to remove them by the municipality was well organized, such as that of squatters near Orlando led by James 'Sofasonke' Mpanza. By 1947 such resistance was weakened, partly by the provision of alternative, albeit inadequate, accommodation (Stadler 1979). Squatter leaders remained significant, however, either in the organization of township gangs or as co-opted local administrators in the 1950s (Bonner 1990b).

Township and squatter protests were matched by another significant development of the 1940s, the emergence of black trade unionism. Semi-skilled and skilled workers both in factories and on the mines acquired greater bargaining power in the post-Depression boom and joined forces with unskilled workers in demanding better wages and working conditions. A number of strikes took place on the Rand and a unified Council for Non-European Trade Unions (CNETU) was formed in 1941.

The failure of the reserves to provide a supplement to mine worker incomes led to demands for better wages, family housing and the end of the migrant labour system (O'Meara 1976). In 1946 a general strike of mine workers took place which mobilized over 70,000 workers throughout the Rand. As in 1922, Smuts suppressed it with ferocity, and with many casualties.

The collapse of the mine workers' strike weakened the CNETU. Nonetheless the strike was a sign of the potential of black labour organization. It also seriously alarmed employers and the white electorate who perceived the threat of the *swart gevaar* (black peril) and who called for tighter influx control. This was a major prop in the apartheid platform of the National Party as it fought the 1948 general election on a campaign of heightened segregation.

SUGGESTIONS FOR FURTHER READING

Beinart, W., Delius, P. and Trapido, S. (eds) 1986: *Putting a plough to the ground: accumulation and dispossession in rural South Africa, 1850–1930.* Johannesburg: Ravan.

Bundy, C. 1979: *The rise and fall of the South African peasantry.* London: Heinemann. 2nd edition, 1988, London: James Currey; Cape Town: David Philip.

Marks, S. and Rathbone, R. (eds) 1982: *Industrialisation and social change in South Africa.* London: Longman.

4

White Supremacy, Segregation and Apartheid

How did South Africa become a society in which racial discrimination was so deeply entrenched?

White racism was certainly not confined to South Africa. Its roots are complex, embedded in the lengthy process of European colonialism, the subjugation of other people in territorial conquest and black enslavement. It was given further impetus from the middle of the nineteenth century when the need to 'civilize inferior natives' became part of the justification for the scramble for Africa. This was also the period when Darwinist notions of evolution and hierarchy were applied to human races. Whites readily came to believe that they were at the top of the evolutionary scale, as shown by their apparent technological superiority and the dynamism of their imperial expansion, while blacks at the bottom were primitive, less intelligent and sluggard. Such pseudo-scientific 'Social Darwinism' clearly fitted the colonizers' view of themselves and their world.

This kind of white supremacism took strong root in South Africa, as it did in other British colonies in Africa and Asia as well as in the United States. But in South Africa it developed into a systematic and legalized discrimination shaping the economic, social and political structure of the whole country in a more pervasive way than elsewhere. And while after 1945 white supremacism began to wane as many colonies began the move towards independence, in South Africa discrimination became even more entrenched. Under 'apartheid', South Africa from the late 1940s diverged from international trends and was marked out for isolation.

This chapter will examine the ways in which racial discrimination in the pre-industrial period developed into structured segregation in the first few decades of the twentieth century, the context in which this evolved into the ideology of apartheid and the varied attempts of a range of organizations to resist these developments.

White supremacism before the twentieth century

The roots of apartheid are much disputed by South African historians. Liberals writing in the early and mid-twentieth century placed emphasis on the irrational frontier prejudices of nineteenth-century Afrikaners; prejudices which came to override liberal non-racialism and were resurrected by the National Party's policy of 1948. Such a view has become widespread amongst English-speaking South Africans and outside the country. But it has obvious flaws. Notably it ignores the racial discrimination of British settlers and officials. And segregation developed before the triumph of Afrikaner political power in 1948.

An alternative view developed in the 1970s is that segregation was the product of the Mineral Revolution, particularly in response to the needs of the mining industry, and that apartheid was built on these foundations. There is certainly much truth in this. However, to neglect the period before the end of the nineteenth century distorts understanding of the context in which segregation developed. Important precedents were created in the pre-industrial period.

Perceptions of white racial superiority were apparent from the earliest colonial encounters of the Dutch settlers with Khoi pastoralists at the Cape. They also acquired a structured form in the divisions of legal status in early Cape society: Dutch East India Company officials, free burghers (settlers), slaves, 'Hottentots' (Khoisan) and Free Blacks (manumitted slaves). The first two categories were made up of whites, the others of blacks. Slavery, which lasted from 1658 to 1834, deeply influenced the class divide of the colony (Worden 1985). All slaves and most labourers were black; landowners and employers were white. There were some exceptions to this rule, since some VOC employees served as overseers on farms and a propertied and slave-owning free black community developed in Cape Town. However, slave manumission levels were low (Elphick and Shell 1989). And although miscegenation existed there was no equivalent to the mixed-race mestizo classes of Latin American colonies where they fulfilled important interstitial positions in the economy. Thus at the Cape 'by the late eighteenth century race and class had overlapped for so long . . . that to many Europeans this social structure appeared to be natural or God-given' (Elphick and Giliomee 1989: 544).

Freund (1976) has argued that these prejudices and the close identification of status and race were not entrenched in the legal order of the early Cape, and cannot be said to have been the precursor of the structured racism of the twentieth century. While the latter point is valid, there were nonetheless a number of racially discriminatory regulations by the end of the eighteenth century. Khoi and slaves were discriminated against in the church and the courts. Free Blacks also faced discriminatory controls, such as liability to arrest if found in the streets of Cape Town without lanterns. None of these rules applied to whites. From the 1760s slaves and Khoi were obliged to carry passes signed by their employers to prove that they were not runaways. In 1809 a proclamation by the British governor Lord Caledon laid down that all 'Hottentots' (Khoi) must have a 'fixed place of abode', normally on a settler farm as a worker. This was to be registered with the local authorities, from whom passes had to be obtained before they could move out of the area. In 1812 Khoi children brought up on settler farms were indentured for ten years until the age of eighteen, thus effectively immobilizing Khoi families on specific farms (Elphick and Malherbe 1989: 40–1).

In contrast to the general identity of race and class in the settled southwestern districts of the early Cape colony, Legassick has argued that 'white frontiersmen expected all their dependents (save their families) to be non-white: they did not expect all non-whites to be their servants' and that 'the frontier in fact provided opportunities for non-whites to which they had no access in the capital' (1980: 56, 67). Links of trade and mutual dependence between settlers and indigenous people were more significant than had been previously acknowledged. This view contradicts the liberal tradition that the remoter pastoral frontier was the cradle of racism. There is a danger of over-stressing the co-operative aspects of frontier life; the crudest examples of coercive violence between settlers and Khoi come from the northern and eastern Cape, and the conflicts of the early nineteenth century with the Xhosa heightened racial hostility. But Legassick's argument does point to the need to probe behind the stereotype of frontier racism.

In the early nineteenth century, important changes took place at the Cape. The commercialization and expansion of the colony required

67

an increase in the supply and mobility of labour. So Ordinance 50 of 1828 removed the controls of passes and indenture over the Khoi, and slavery was ended in 1834 (although slaves remained apprenticed to their owners until 1838). These measures did not greatly affect the material conditions of proletarianized freed slaves and Khoi, most of whom lacked access to land and capital, although they did permit their movement to new employers. In racial terms the removal of the distinction between slaves and Khoi led to the identification of them more broadly as 'coloured', in contrast to the 'white' and 'Native' inhabitants of the colony.

Legislation was also passed in 1828 to deal with the use of African labourers. Ordinance 49 permitted Africans to enter the colony, but stated that they were subject to arrest if they were found without a pass issued on their arrival or if they failed to enter employment. As Hindson has pointed out, this contrasts with the use of passes in the 1809 Caledon Code which was intended to immobilize existing workers and prevent them from moving in search of alternative work. Ordinance 49 encouraged workers to enter the colony and to search for employers in a more mobile labour market, although it still enforced compulsory labour penalties for 'vagrants' or those who were unemployed. It thus 'reflects the beginning of a transition from servile to market allocated labour, albeit on a limited scale' (Hindson 1987: 17).

However, other key laws in the mid-nineteenth-century Cape made no reference to race. For instance, the Masters and Servants Ordinance of 1841, designed to regulate labour contracts, was colour blind. Legislation with overtly racial controls, such as the proposed Vagrancy Ordinance of 1834, was vetoed. Most significantly the franchise established for the Cape Town municipality in 1839 and that for representative government in 1853 were not racially defined. These acts were far from socially disruptive: in practice most servants under the Masters and Servants regulations were black and almost all masters were white. The 1853 franchise was based on earnings and property ownership, although these were set at quite low levels: earnings of £50 a year or property, which included land, worth £25. This admitted a number of coloured and African voters, as well as a large proportion of the Afrikaner males in the colony (Lewsen 1971).

The non-racial franchise lay at the core of mid-nineteenth-century Cape liberalism. Like liberal constitutions in Europe at the time, it abolished monopoly of power by right of birth and ancestry but it upheld the interests of men of property and wealth. Yet Cape liberalism was more than just an import from mid-Victorian Britain. Trapido (1980) has argued that it must be seen in the context of the particular social formation of the Cape. It went further in its low franchise qualifications than most other constitutions of its time by incorporating many 'small men' whose interests were nonetheless linked to the administrative and commercial ruling classes. These included black ('coloured' and African) peasant farmers whose votes could be relied upon to support commercial development but it excluded the proletarianized labourers.

This class-based analysis of Cape liberalism is also used to explain its apparent decline in the late nineteenth century. By the 1880s, peasant production was less favoured, and small-scale commercial interests were giving way to larger capital interests. Moreover, the incorporation of the Ciskei in 1865 and the Transkeian territories twenty or so years later threatened to alter the balance of power by enfranchising large numbers of African landowners. As a result higher franchise qualifications and literacy tests were introduced. Overtly discriminatory Acts were passed in the 1880s and 1890s, such as the anti-squatting legislation and the Glen Grey Act (see p. 48). The latter not only restricted individual land tenure but also set up district councils under appointed local chiefs and headmen to administer specified areas of African cultivation. The system spread from the eastern Cape into some Transkeian districts and Pondoland in 1905 and 1911. Rich (1981) has argued that it had an important influence on the segregationist notions of separate reserve administration in the 1920s.

By the turn of the century, some Cape legislation was overtly racial. Liquor laws restricted the sale of alcohol to Africans in the Transkeian territories and elsewhere. More fundamentally, a segregated location was established for Africans in Cape Town in 1902. In 1905 the School Board Act introduced compulsory educational segregation. It is true, as Lewsen has pointed out (1983), that in some other respects racial integration existed at the Cape at a greater level than elsewhere (for instance in the early trade union movement in Cape Town and in government service). Nonetheless Cape liberalism was certainly dented by 1910. The Act of Union preserved the Cape franchise in that province, but there was no concerted attempt by the Cape representatives to have it extended elsewhere. And even in the Cape the black franchise remained limited by property qualifications while for whites under the Act of Union it included all adult males. Africans were also not permitted to stand as parliamentary candidates but were to be represented by whites. As Davenport has noted, 'even liberals were more concerned in the final resort to preserve the dignity of the Cape in its relations with the other colonies than the rights of blacks' (1987: 33).

In fact white supremacist notions were heightened in the mid-nineteenth-century period at the time of the origins of Cape liberalism. In the 1830s racist arguments were used by those calling for vagrancy legislation and controls over slave apprentices. And although the underlying causes of the Great Trek were economic (see p. 12), one of the stated objections of the emigrants had been the placing of slaves on an 'equal footing . . . contrary to the . . . natural distinction of race and colour'.

The principles of the Cape liberal franchise were clearly rejected in the constitutions of the trekker republics. The very concept of citizenship was defined by membership of trekker families, since isolated farmers and settlers attempted to establish forms of government in regions where indigenous people were still occupying much of the land. Thus there were no limitations of property or wealth as at the Cape, but political representation was restricted racially to whites. The 1839 constitution of Natalia laid down annual elections for all adult white males. The successor trekker republics in the Free State and the Transvaal followed this pattern. The Transvaal *grondwet* (constitution) of 1858 stated explicitly that 'the people desire to permit no equality between coloured people and the white inhabitants of the country, either in church or state'.

This was also clear in other aspects of the trekker polities. The Dutch Reformed Church (DRC) resolved to segregate its churches in 1857, a move which led inexorably in 1881 to the complete separation of the established DRC for whites and the Sendingkerk (Mission Church) for everyone else (Ritner 1967). And political power remained confined to whites. Indians were excluded from the Free State altogether, and in the Transvaal were denied the franchise in the 1880s. Yet the issue here was not just one of black exclusion. One of the bones of contention in the Transvaal in the 1890s was the refusal of Kruger's government to give representation to white outsiders (uitlanders).

Other discriminatory Acts in the republics were passed, although often without the means of effective enforcement. Africans were forbidden to carry guns and they were subject to vagrancy and pass laws. In the Free State they were not permitted to register land ownership, although many controlled land held nominally by missionaries and other whites, and in the Transvaal some land was purchased by African chiefs in the years after the South African War. In the 1870s and 1880s, the lure of the mines led to stricter enforcement of pass laws by the state in an attempt to keep labour on the farms.

But these policies were not confined to the Boer republics, as is illustrated by the position in Natal. Initially the charter granted to the colony in 1856 did set up a non-racial franchise on the lines of that of the Cape, granting a vote to those with fixed property worth £50 or those paying £10 per annum in rent. However, once the Natal settlers gained control over government, this was whittled down. As more and more Africans acquired claims to land which brought them within these levels, laws stemming black registration were quickly passed in the 1860s. Moves were also made to exclude Indians, many of whom were merchants and men of property, from the franchise, although this was not finally achieved until 1896.

Overtly racial controls were also established by such means as the levy of a £3 poll tax on all Indian labour immigrants who remained in Natal without renewing their indentures. African migrants entering the colony from the 1860s were obliged to carry passes, in a measure very similar to the Cape Ordinance 49. And by the time of Union settler racist hysteria had reached a height in the aftermath of the Bambatha rebellion and Indian protest actions. Natal fitted happily into the Union's racially restricted franchise.

Natal was also the site of what Welsh (1971) has described as South Africa's first example of structured segregation: a form of indirect rule over Africans known as the 'Shepstone system'. Shepstone was placed in charge of 'Native Affairs' in the colony in 1846. Given the weakness of the settlers, he realized that the only way to protect the colonial state was to allocate land still unclaimed by white farmers as 'locations' which Africans would have the right to cultivate undisturbed, under the rule of local headmen and chiefs operating under 'Native Law', although this was ill defined. Control over the chiefs was in the hands of white Resident Magistrates and Administrators of Native Law, themselves subject to Shepstone and the Natal Legislative Council. Crucial to this system were the hut taxes that were levied on each head of household. These paid for the administration of not only the locations but also of much of settler Natal (Etherington 1989).

The Shepstone system was opposed by poorer settler farmers who resented the tying up of land and labour in the locations. However, as labour became more readily available with external migration in the

1870s and 1880s such complaints died down. Shepstone and his supporters claimed that the system of separation existed to 'protect' Africans from erosion of their society by European influences, particularly in matters of land tenure and homestead production. However, it is clear that his motivation was primarily protection of the colony against the instability of African competition and 'disorder'. The priority of control was evident in the curfews and pass laws used to restrict Africans working in towns and villages outside the locations. And the contrast of the stability of Natal with the upheavals of neighbouring Zululand served to bolster this view of the Shepstone system amongst the white settlers.

By the time of Union Natalians were therefore firmly behind the principle of segregation. Shepstonian notions of separate administrative and legal systems had much influence on the development of 'Native' policy in the Union in the 1920s, as we shall see. Other foundations of segregation in the early twentieth century had precedents in the white supremacist laws and practices of the nineteenth century. However, it was not until the early twentieth century that a concerted ideology and over-arching plan of segregation was developed.

Segregation

Segregation needs to be distinguished from white supremacy. Although it was predicated on perceptions of racial difference and was developed in the aftermath of colonial conquest, South African segregation was not just racial subordination writ large. Its underlying principle was the enforced separation, not just subordination, of blacks and whites in the spheres of work, residence and government. Nineteenth-century precedents for this had been seen in the demarcation of land and authority set up under the Glen Grey Act in the eastern Cape and the Shepstone system in Natal. But it was only in the period between the end of the South African War in 1902 and the 1930s that a cogent ideology of segregation emerged and was implemented.

There has been some disagreement amongst historians as to precisely when and why segregation emerged. The liberal view that it was a direct heritage of the nineteenth-century Boer Republics has now been repudiated. Indeed the Transvaal and Orange Free State were less racially segregated in terms of land settlement and economic activity than were Natal and the eastern Cape. As Cell has pointed out, the Boer General Botha, who was to become the first Prime Minister of the Union, stated in 1903 that cheap African labour was needed on the farms, not segregated tribal reserves which locked up labour and withheld land from white ownership. White supremacy was certainly central to his thinking but 'the language and the details of segregation would represent not a direct continuation of prevailing Afrikaner ideas about how economy and society should be regulated, but a distinct departure from them' (Cell 1982: 49).

Botha's comments were made in testimony he gave to the South African Native Affairs Commission (SANAC), appointed by Milner, which sat between 1903 and 1905. Its function was to prepare the way for Union by establishing outline policies for Africans. As Cell has shown, its major recommendations provided the first clear articulation of segregationist ideals and it was the blueprint for much of the legislation that followed Union. Thus it proposed racial separation of land ownership, the establishment of 'Native locations' in towns, regulation of labour influx to the cities with pass laws, differential wage levels, mission-based schooling for Africans rather than state education, administration in separate Native Councils and no extension of the Cape's non-racial franchise to other parts of the Union.

Some of these recommendations were based on existing practices in various parts of the country, such as pass laws, urban locations and racially determined wage levels. But it was only during Milner's Reconstruction administration that they were combined into an over-arching general policy.

As we have seen in the previous chapter, many of the recommendations of the SANAC were put into practice by legislation of the subsequent decades. Most notable were the Mines and Works Act (1911), which imposed the colour bar, the Natives Land Act (1913), which segregated land ownership, and the Natives (Urban Areas) Act (1923), which provided for residential segregation in towns.

In addition to these restrictions, Africans had long been subject to a variety of pass controls, requiring them to obtain official documents in order to move freely between town and countryside. The Stallard doctrine of controlled urbanization (see p. 43) required such mechanisms to be extended, although women were exempted after the effective resistance to passes for women mounted in the Orange Free State in 1913. During the 1930s and 1940s attempts were made to tighten up pass laws, although it was not until the 1950s that they were centralized in a single administrative system.

Another key element in segregationist policy was the Native Affairs Act (1920), which set up separate tribal councils for the administration of the reserves and advisory councils for Africans in urban areas, all under the aegis of the Native Affairs Department and under the ultimate authority of the Prime Minister. Administrative segregation was the logical development of the denial of African political representation in the central bodies of government in the Union. And finally the Industrial Conciliation Act (1924) legalized the collective bargaining power of trade unions, but excluded migrant workers from its definition of 'employee'. This was a clear attempt by the Smuts government to woo white workers after the Rand Revolt, but when the government was ousted by the Labour–National Party 'Pact' in 1924 it was clear that this policy had not worked.

The basic tenets of segregation were thus laid down under the Smuts government. However, under Hertzog's Pact administration segregationism continued with renewed vitality. The Labour Party's demand for white worker protection, forged in the conflicts of the Rand, was extended to other areas of employment. Creswell, the Labour Party leader and new Minister of Labour, replaced Africans with white workers in major areas of government employment such as the railways, harbours and post offices. This was extended under the 1926 Mines and Works Amendment Act which gave the government powers of colour bar enforcement in private industry. Moreover, this 'civilized labour policy' established racial differences in wage rates between 'persons whose standard of living conforms to the standard of living generally recognised as tolerable from the usual European standpoint' and others 'whose aim is restricted to the barer requirements of the necessities of life as understood among barbarous and under-developed peoples'.

A further major segregationist measure of the Pact government related to the administration of the reserves. The Native Administration Act (1927) stressed the need for Africans to be retribalized under a distinct system of law and government. A more uniform system of administration was applied, with chiefs responsible for paying the taxes of the Africans under their control and subject to a more codified single system of 'Native Law'. The Native Affairs Department was given a more regulatory role, which included disciplining chiefs and the possibility of relocating communities to fit the government's notions of ethnic distribution within the reserves.

The 1927 Act marked a rejection of the notion of political assimilation of Africans into the Union. It clearly backed the Natal principles of bolstering 'traditional' authorities in the reserves under the 'Supreme Chief', the Governor-General of South Africa, in ways which resembled the old Shepstonian system. Its conscious revival of tribalism, although bearing no resemblance to any pre-colonial structure, was to be crucially important to the development of diverse African ethnicities which were brought to full fruition in the homelands policy of the 1960s (see pp. 110–13).

As another part of the move to entrench tribalism, an assault was made on the Cape enfranchisement of detribalized African property owners. In 1926 Hertzog introduced a series of bills into Parliament proposing the removal of individual voters from the electoral roll, to be replaced by a limited number of white representatives chosen by chiefs and headmen. Partial compensation was to be provided by the establishment of a Natives Representative Council, although this was also dominated by chiefs and headmen and had only limited advisory powers. However, under the Union constitution such a change to the franchise required a two-thirds majority in Parliament. This was not obtained until Hertzog's National Party fused with Smuts to form the United Party in the 1933 government. In 1936 the Representation of Natives Act was finally passed, removing the Cape franchise. It was partially driven through by the 'compensation' of extending the reserve areas in the Native Trust and Land Act (see p. 60). Segregation of African administration and political power was now complete.

Each of these pieces of legislation had its own specific context. But what underlay the broad segregationist thrust that united them all?

The consensus amongst revisionist historians of the 1970s and 1980s was that segregation represented the entrenchment of the cheap labour policies developed in the mines of Kimberley and the Rand in the early stages of the Mineral Revolution. The SANAC met during a period of considerable uncertainty after the upheavals of the South African War had led to decreased migrant labour supplies as a result of the 'rolling back' of the territorial conquest of Africans (see p. 30). Under these circumstances Milner's Reconstruction administration was primarily concerned with establishing a firm foundation for the mining industry. Seen in this light, the SANAC recommendations show the extent to which segregation was a product of the particular circumstances of South Africa's Mineral Revolution. Thus the principle of migrant labour, with subsistence in rural areas, was to be entrenched and permanent urbanization leading to high wage demands would be checked by influx controls.

In the subsequent decades the pre-eminence of the mining industry gave way to other interest groups whose votes influenced the policy of the unified state in the direction of segregation. Notable amongst these were white farmers needing both cheap labour and monopoly of land ownership to meet the opportunities of an industrializing society, and white workers demanding protectionist employment and wages. Hertzog's legislation reflected these forces (Lacey 1981).

There is no doubt that segregation was the product of South Africa's industrial revolution. But there is a danger of seeing it as a rigid and uniform policy enforced by the state in the interests of mine owners, white workers and farmers. More recently some historians have examined the complexity of segregationist thinking and the circumstances in which it took root. Dubow has pointed out that before the 1920s, although key items of segregationist legislation were introduced, they 'were seldom interpreted as integral elements of a united ideological package' (1989: 39). The SANAC recommendations were not adopted wholesale, and implementation of segregation was still very patchy. The division of land was still incomplete after the 1913 Land Act, proposals made in 1917 for administrative segregation were dropped and much uncertainty surrounded 'Native Policy' in the period of heightened conflict on the Rand between 1918 and 1922. Permanently proletarianized black workers were growing in number, including on the mines, and the future of the migrant labour system was by no means secure by 1920.

It was only in the 1920s that segregationist ideology became firmly entrenched, particularly in the emphasis on retribalization. In addition, legislation acquired a much more overtly racist character. For instance, in addition to the measures outlined above, the Hertzog administration passed Acts limiting mixed marriages and placed increasingly stringent controls over the mobility and property rights of Indians.

This was not solely a response to the needs of white employers for cheap labour. It was also a reaction to the heightened conflicts of the 1920s, marked by worker militancy, rural resistance, millenarianism and the dramatic growth of the Industrial and Commercial Workers' Union (ICU) (see pp. 52–6). In an important case study demonstrating this argument, Marks (1978) showed how Natal planters in the 1920s came to support the idea of bolstering the Zulu royal chief in a separate administrative structure, in sharp contrast to settler opposition to traditional rulers in the aftermath of the Bambatha rebellion. The reason was the desire to bolster a more conservative system as a means of social control against the alarming alternative focus of the radical ICU.

Dubow has extended this to stress that the recreation of communal land and legal control under chiefs and headmen was intended primarily to stem the threat of an increasingly radicalized African proletariat. Thus Heaton Nicholls, Member of Parliament for Zululand and a key framer of the 1926 Native Bills, stated in their defence that 'if we do not get back to communalism we will most certainly arrive very soon at communism' (Dubow 1989: 71). In his campaigns of the late 1920s Hertzog linked the threat of black 'Bolshevism' with African permanent urbanization and detribalization. In his election speeches of 1929 the 'Black Peril' theme was his key defence of segregation.

The 'Black Peril' slogan tapped a strong underlying current of white supremacism which had certainly not diminished since the late nineteenth century. For instance, opposition to miscegenation and fears of white 'degeneration' in unsegregated cities were widely held notions. Together with this came the belief that Africans were innately incapable of becoming fully incorporated members of 'civilized' society.

Certainly this strong element of racism primarily explains the voter support which segregation received in the 1920s. However, by no means were all segregationists racist fanatics. Indeed, to many influential writers and spokesmen in the early twentieth century, segregation was not only a rejection of the Cape assimilationist tradition but also of overt forms of racial subordination. A new form of pro-segregationist liberalism was emerging which stressed the need to preserve and protect traditional African culture against the onslaught of industrial society. Thus, for instance, Howard Pim, a friend and adviser of Milner, stressed the need to enable the African to live 'under natural conditions which he understands and has created for himself', distant from the disintegrating effects of proletarianization in the towns (Rich 1984: 5). And Ernest Stubbs, Native Commissioner in the eastern Transvaal, believed that segregation would be a means of protecting Africans from white land encroachment (Rich 1980).

Such views were not so much the outcome of concepts of biological racial inferiority as a positive assertion of the values of an existence which their proponents believed was traditionally African. They were strongly influenced by anthropological studies which developed in South Africa in the 1910s and 1920s and which presented the image of a cohesive and unchanging African rural culture (Dubow 1987). Thus academics such as Edgar Brookes, later a vocal critic of apartheid, acted as advisor to Hertzog and strongly supported the 1926 Native Bills on the grounds that they protected Africans from detribalization. Such views were highly influential and were shared by many administrators in the Native Affairs Department. And in his 1929 lectures at Oxford, Smuts, although in parliamentary opposition to Hertzog, gave firm support for protectionist segregation. He rejected both the view of 'the African as essentially inferior' and the assimilationist approach which destroyed 'the basis of his African system which was his highest good'. The solution, he believed, was segregation. 'The new policy . . . is to foster an indigenous native culture or system of cultures, and to cease to force the African into alien European moulds.' Segregation was to replace both assimilation and repression (Dubow 1987: 84).

It was on these grounds that many local Native Affairs Department officials accepted the principles of separate administration, particularly those who had experienced the protectionist mould of the old 'Transkeian' system of indirect rule. However, there were major problems with this kind of justification for segregation. Firstly African societies had never been unchanging and static. The notion of 'traditional culture' embodied in codes of 'native law' and chiefly authorities was as much a creation of early twentieth-century academics and administrators as anything else. Secondly, by the 1920s the reserves were clearly incapable of maintaining any separate political and social order. The process of colonial conquest, new taxes and long exposure to migrant labour, together with land deterioration and general impoverishment, made a mockery of the idealized perception that they could be a repository of a 'traditional' way of life for all Africans. The breakdown of the pre-colonial polities had gone too far to turn the clock back.

By the end of the 1920s many of the liberal segregationists were coming to realize this and were changing their minds. Most prominently, Edgar Brookes made a public recantation in 1927, and others such as Pim followed suit. Hertzog's insistence on overt racial discrimination, marked particularly by the job colour bar, was one source of disillusionment. Some administrators objected to the way in which the 1927 Native Administration Act turned the

Native Affairs Department into a repressive bureaucratic body which broke with the older paternalistic traditions (Dubow 1986). The repressive nature of forced segregation was becoming too evident to ignore.

By the mid-1930s and the 1940s the close interdependence of Africans and urban employers rendered protectionist segregation an invalid notion. Liberal attention diverted away from the hopes of preserving an idealized African lifestyle in the reserves to issues of social welfare in the slums of the cities. That segregation was racial exploitation became crystal clear. The foundation of the Liberal Party in opposition to apartheid in 1953 showed that many earlier supporters of segregation had made an about turn.

The ideology of segregation thus emerged in the context of an industrializing society, founded on specific practices which at the turn of the century had been primarily associated with the mining industry. Although legislative foundations such as the job colour bar, the Land Act and urban segregation were responses to specific white class interests, by the 1920s segregation was primarily intended to prevent African proletarianization which both threatened 'traditional culture' and led to radicalization and overt conflict.

Segregation was thus a complex response to the circumstances of early twentieth-century South Africa. It was not inevitable, nor was it immutable. In the 1940s, it began to break down as the number of Africans moving permanently to the cities grew and as calls were increasingly made for their integration into South Africa outside the reserves. Only with the development of apartheid was a policy found to resurrect it, albeit in a rather different form and with no remnant of the liberal protectionist notion. But before examining the roots of apartheid we need to see how segregation was viewed by those who were at its receiving end.

Black responses to segregation

In the previous chapter we examined many examples of local conflicts in town and countryside during the early decades of South Africa's industrialization. Here we shall look at the broader political and organizational responses of blacks to segregation between the late nineteenth century and the 1940s. This period has often been seen as that of the foundation and growth of African nationalism, although there is a danger of portraying an ever-strengthening and unified

79

national movement. There was much diversity and fluctuation in the development of black political movements.

The roots of African political organization have often been traced to the foundation of the African National Congress in 1912. However, as Odendaal (1984) has shown, black protest politics had a long tradition before then. The earliest examples of black political organizations were found in the eastern Cape in the late nineteenth century where the franchise involved the propertied in politics, led by a mission-educated elite. Competition for African votes became marked in the 1880s when rival political parties encouraged voter registration, and black political activity was marked by petitions, mass meetings and newspapers (Saunders 1970). Organizations such as the Native Educational Association (1879) and Imbumba ya Manyama (Union of Black People) (1882) were founded to air issues of particular concern to black voters. Their membership strongly over-lapped with those involved in the electoral committees, agents' meetings and registration campaigns that surrounded the political parties.

Political divisions soon emerged. A key figure was John Tengo Jabavu, a mission-educated teacher whose support for independent political candidates gave backing for his newspaper *Imvo Zabantsundu* (Native Opinion). Through it strong protests were registered at the increase in the franchise qualifications of 1887 and other grievances of the African middle class. However, by the 1890s Jabavu's support for Afrikaner Bond candidates led to the founding of an alternative newspaper *Izwi Labantu* (Voice of the Black People) and the formation of the South African Native Congress, with leading members based in East London and led by the cleric Walter Rubusana and magistrate Allan Soga. The Congress grew in membership and organization with many local area branches and it became the main focus of Cape African political expression in the period around and following the South African War, with strongly pro-British sympathies.

Despite the lack of constitutional outlets for black political involvement in the other parts of South Africa, organizations did emerge in the heightened political atmosphere of the South African War. The Natal Native Congress, led by the teacher and minister John Dube, provided an outlet for the aspirations of the kholwa landowning class with its newspaper *Ilanga lase Natal* (Natal Sun). Similar though smaller groupings also arose in the Free State and the Transvaal, and other African newspapers appeared, such as Sol Plaatje's *Sesotho Tsala ea Batho* (Friend of the People).

80

Despite regional and political differences African political involvement before 1910 was characterized by a liberalism which reflected the position of the African elite within colonial society, and which had little contact with more populist rural protest movements such as Transkei protests against taxation or the Bambatha revolt. Mission-educated and predominantly middle-class professionals, the members of such bodies called for equal access to education and an extension of the Cape's limited black franchise to other parts of the country, but they accepted the paternalism of white society. Thus the executive of the South African Native Congress reassured the British Colonial Secretary in 1903 that the formation of independent African churches should not be seen as a challenge to white ecclesiastical and government authority, since

> the black races are too conscious of their dependence upon the white missionaries and of their obligations towards the British race, and the benefits to be derived by their presence in the general control and guidance of the civil and religious affairs of the country to harbour foolish notions of political ascendency.
>
> (Karis and Carter 1973: vol. 1, 18)

This co-operative stance was clear in the approval given by the SANAC (1903–5) of the open conduct of African political activities, which presented little threat to the status quo.

However, African disillusionment with the benefits of colonial rule began to set in shortly after this. The failure of the Union constitution to extend the Cape's non-racial franchise led to fruitless petitions and appeals to both the local and British administrations. The optimism of the 1890s was shattered. Segregationist legislation of the early Union government, notably the Mines and Works Act and the Natives Land Bill, showed that African interests could not be served by influencing white politicians on an individual basis, and this acted as a catalyst for more permanent organised unity. Delegates from throughout South Africa met in 1912 in Bloemfontein to form the South African Native National Congress (SANNC) (renamed the African National Congress (ANC) in 1923).

The declared intention of the SANNC as set out in its first constitution was

> to encourage mutual understanding and to bring together into common action as one political people all tribes and clans of

various tribes or races and by means of combined effort and united political organization to defend their freedom, rights and privileges.

(Karis and Carter 1973: vol. 1, 77)

However, it was far from a mass movement. It included some of the main chiefs and rural leaders, but its members were still primarily middle-class men who feared 'being thrust back into the ranks of the urban and rural poor' by the legislation of the post-Union years (Lodge 1983: 2).

The tactics of the SANNC were accordingly moderate. It still hoped to exert influence by petitions, delegations and journalism. Thus opposition to the Land Act was epitomized by the writing of its secretary Sol Plaatje and by a delegation of protest to London. There was little contact with popular protests such as the pass burning campaigns in Bloemfontein or the labour disputes of the Rand. Loyalty to the British Empire was still stressed, and shown by the suspension of all protest during the First World War.

The ineffectiveness of such approaches became clear by the end of the decade. In the years following the end of the war, a diversity of African elite political responses emerged. Congress's leader, Dube, cautiously accepted the principle of segregation, although objecting to the unfairness of the terms of the Land Act. This led to his ousting from the presidency, but he remained in control of the Natal branch of Congress. In this influential position he stressed the need for black self-help education rather than challenges to the state, in a tradition which owed much to his experience of Booker Washington's ideas during a visit to the United States. The Natal Congress was dominated by kholwa landowners who came to actively support the re-establishment of the Zulu monarchy and the principle of Zulu ethnic nationalism, symbolized by the founding of Inkatha ka Zulu in 1922–3 as a conservative bulwark against the radicalism of the ICU (Marks 1986a: 36–7). Dube and his supporters seemed to follow the pro-segregationist stance of the liberal protectionists, a position which was particularly strongly held in Natal.

By contrast, in the Transvaal a section of the Congress leaders did identify with the more radical labour movement on the Rand. There they faced common grievances of low wages, inadequate housing and tightening of the pass laws. As a result they gave support to the striking municipal workers in Johannesburg in 1918 and to the anti-pass campaigns of the following year, and showed sympathy to the mineworkers' strike of 1920 (Bonner 1982). However, this class alliance was always precarious and Congress leadership was never wholly in favour of strike action and always nervous of a mass uprising. With the suppression of the 1920 strike, ANC leaders distanced themselves from the 'Bolshevism' of labour protest. Vaguely conciliatory moves on the part of the government, such as an enquiry into the pass laws and labour issues, were sufficient to disengage them from the main body of protesters.

Co-operation with employers is also apparent in Willan's case study of Sol Plaatje's relations with the monopoly de Beers mining company in Kimberley in 1918–19 (1978). De Beers gave active support to Plaatje's self-improving and Christian-based 'Brotherhood movement' in a clear bid to keep out 'the black Bolsheviks of Johannesburg'. As this example shows, Congress support for worker protest was limited to the Rand.

Congress alienation from popular protest continued into the 1920s. Many middle-class African leaders followed Dube's example and were involved in joint deliberations with the liberal segregationists, rejecting the radicalism of the ICU and the millenarianism of rural protests such as the Wellington movement. However, the Hertzog Bills of 1926 to remove the Cape African franchise gave them a shock, and revealed the barrenness of a segregationism which sought to recreate a tribalism from which they were far removed. This led to some reconciliation with other movements. J. Gumede, elected as president of Congress in 1927, was much influenced by Garveyism as well as open to contact with the Communist Party of South Africa (CPSA). The way to this had been opened by the CPSA's temporary re-orientation from white worker mobilization to acceptance of co-operation with reformist middle class organizations such as Congress. The heightened tensions of the 1929 'Black Peril' election gave further meaning to such an alliance.

However, by 1930 the Communist Party had again withdrawn from such contacts, and a more conservative backlash in Congress was shown when Gumede was voted out of office and replaced by Pixley Seme. In the 1930s the ANC went into sharp decline. Its cautious and conservative orientation towards the reserve chiefs and the aspiring African commercial and middle classes provided little link with the majority of the population facing rural impoverishment and urban proletarianization. Militants in the organization were expelled and it lapsed into almost total inactivity.

Broadly similar patterns of class representation and tactics can be identified in the political organization of other South Africans who were threatened by segregationist measures. By the end of the nineteenth century a sense of 'coloured' identity was growing, particularly in Cape Town and amongst the professional classes who were facing ostracism from white racism but were concerned to distance themselves from Africans, who were subject to greater discrimination, and to claim rights to full participation in 'civilized' society (Goldin 1987). In 1902 members of the coloured elite, concerned at the establishment of an African location in Cape Town and the application of pass laws to Africans which they feared might come to be applied to them, founded the African Political (later People's) Organization (APO). Under the leadership of Abdullah Abdurahman, a member of the Cape Town City Council, the APO protested strongly against the provision of compulsory state education for whites only as well as the lack of enfranchisement of coloureds outside the Cape.

However, as with the SANNC, there were limits to how far the APO was prepared to go. It showed little support for radical action, much faith in British liberal principles and overt support for the British cause in the First World War. In the early 1920s the APO organized petitions against increasing discrimination, but these were ignored by the government and the organization was seen to be increasingly irrelevant to both the radical trade union movement representing coloured workers and to the more conservative coloured middle class. The APO did nothing to back the campaign to support farm worker strikes in the western Cape against low wages in the late 1920s. Hopes that coloureds would be given a 'new deal' were raised by one of Hertzog's 1926 bills which confirmed coloured voting rights in the Cape and proposed its extension to the whole Union, in contrast to the disenfranchisement of Africans. APO opposition to segregationism was consequently weakened. By 1936, when Hertzog no longer needed coloured voting support, this bill was dropped. The APO could offer little effective protest (Lewis 1987).

Another focus for political organization amongst the disenfranchised lay amongst the Indian population of Natal and the Transvaal. Early organizations established in both regions in the 1890s represented the commercial classes, opposed to franchise restrictions and trading limitations but making no contact with the grievances of Indian indentured labourers and their descendants. Between 1906 and 1914 greater radicalization did develop, and passive resistance campaigns, largely organized by Mahatma Gandhi, opposed regis-

84

tration taxes and other discriminatory legislation. In 1913, such campaigns briefly linked up with a general strike of rural workers. But then splits again emerged, partly because of Gandhi's departure for India, but also because the commercial elite who dominated both the Natal and Transvaal Indian Congress consciously distanced themselves from worker radicalism, particularly as represented in the late 1920s by support of Indian workers for the ICU (Swan 1987).

It was only in the mid-1930s with the implementation of the Hertzog bills that a revival of organizational opposition took place and a new bid for unified action was made. In 1935 over 400 delegates from a variety of organizations, including Jabavu, Seme, leaders of the Communist Party, the APO and the South African Indian Congress, met together and formed the All African Convention (AAC). Again, the delegates were primarily professional and middle-class men, who were now alienated from the repressive segregationism of the Hertzog years. The AAC's tactics of petition and moderate reformism, however, differed little from earlier methods and it met with as little response from the government as did the SANNC in 1912.

The failings of the AAC and other organizations to meet the challenge of segregation led to the emergence of more radical breakaway groupings. In the western Cape disillusionment with the inactivity and reformism of the APO led to the foundation of the National Liberation League (NLL), led by Abdurahman's daughter, 'Cissie' Gool, a prominent member of the Communist Party. Disgusted by the AAC's refusal to boycott segregated administrative structures, the NLL called for a national organization to protest more radically against segregation. The Non-European United Front was the result, which during the Second World War renamed as the Non-European Unity Movement and produced the 'Ten Point Programme' (1943) identifying the 'present system in South Africa' as 'similar to the Nazi system of Herrenvolk', and calling for a united stand of all opposed to segregation and the establishment of democracy as the rule 'of the people, by the people, for the people' (Karis and Carter 1973: vol. 2, 352–7).

The background to this process of radicalization was not only disillusionment with the failings of existing organizations but also the upsurge of popular protest which emerged in the 1940s (see pp. 63–4). At last this found resonance in black political organizations.

The ANC had undergone some revival with reorganization and an active membership recruitment campaign under Alfred Xuma, elected president in 1940. At the same time, younger members of the ANC, less imbued with respect for white authority and chiefly power than their elders and concerned with the failure of Congress to respond to the urban and labour protests, challenged the orientation of the organization. The Congress Youth League, formed in 1943 under the leadership of Anton Lembede, stressed the importance of African leadership and self-determination, the need to 'go down to the masses' and the importance of such direct action as boycotts, strikes and trade union mobilization. This marked a sharp break with the deferential policies and practices of the ANC in the 1930s. Some of the Youth League leaders, such as Lembede, Walter Sisulu, Oliver Tambo and Nelson Mandela, were elected to the executive alongside older-style liberals and Communist Party members. In general, however, the Youth Leaguers were suspicious of the intentions of the white-dominated Communist Party. Lembede in particular stressed the need for African control over political ideology, thus anticipating the black consciousness developments of subsequent decades, although after his early death in 1947 some of the cohesion of his political philosophy was weakened. Nonetheless, the Youth Leaguers had moved beyond the view of their Congress predecessors that African nationalism meant black unity as one part of a wider South Africa. For them Africans were by right of their indigenous status and numerical preponderance the only people entitled to rule South Africa (Gerhart 1978: 67).

Events after the Second World War gave further impetus to more militant strategies. Popular protest continued, marked by strikes on the Rand and in Durban. Indian passive resistance campaigns were renewed in the Transvaal and Natal against the Ghetto Act, which limited areas of Indian property ownership. In this way the leadership of the South African Indian Congress was mobilized together with wider worker support and ANC, Unity Movement and Communist Party sympathies. Such events as these brought some international condemnation of the Smuts government, with the newly independent India breaking off economic and diplomatic ties in the first example of sanctions against South Africa, although the United Nations refused to condemn what it regarded as matters of internal policy.

The example of national determination provided by the independence of India in 1947 and set out in the 1941 Atlantic Charter influenced the Youth Leaguers of the ANC. Moreover, they faced the threat of white demands for the rigid imposition of segregation, a threat brought to reality in the victory of the National Party in 1948 under its slogan of apartheid.

Against this background the Youth League produced its Programme of Action (1949) which marked a decisive break with the conciliatory policies of the previous decades. It called for 'national freedom' and political independence from white domination, a sign of the influence of Lembede's Africanism, together with rejection of all forms of segregation and the use of weapons of boycott, civil disobedience and strike. These tactics reflected the changing membership of Congress and the final recognition that segregation had to be counteracted at the popular level and by more drastic means than those used previously. The problem was that opponents of discrimination now faced a newly determined segregationist government.

Afrikaner nationalism and apartheid

Apartheid emerged as the slogan of the Gesuiwerde Nasionale Party (later renamed the Herenigde Nasionale Party (HNP)), which originated as a splinter group from Hertzog's National Party in 1934 and captured leadership of political Afrikanerdom in the 1940s. In 1948 the HNP narrowly won power. Apartheid had been a means by which it drew voters together behind a revived Afrikaner nationalist political movement.

Afrikaner nationalism is a topic surrounded by mythology. Like all nationalist movements it has created its own symbolism and its own history stressing the unified experience of the Afrikaner *volk*: born on the old Cape frontier, trekking away from the British in 1836, surviving attacks by hostile Africans in the interior, defending themselves against the British in the 1870s and again in the South African War, suffering maltreatment in British concentration camps, rebelling against South African support for the British cause in the First World War, partially triumphing in the 1920s under the Hertzog government which made Afrikaans an official language, reacting against the English-dominated Fusion government of Hertzog and Smuts in the 1930s and early 1940s, finally winning the election of 1948 and – the ultimate achievement – breaking from the Commonwealth and establishing a republic in 1961.

Certainly all of these events took place. But such a one-track view ignores the diversity of experience of Afrikaners of different regions and classes. The notion of Afrikaner nationalism had to be consciously forged rather than growing spontaneously. In this it did not differ from other nationalist movements in nineteenth-century Europe or indeed from African nationalism in South Africa. Apartheid was an important means by which political unity was forged out of Afrikaner diversity in the 1940s.

Like African political consciousness, Afrikaner nationalism was rooted in the experience and leadership of middle-class teachers and clerics in the late nineteenth-century Cape, although in its western rather than eastern region. A group of them in Paarl founded the Genootskap van Regte Afrikaners (Society of True Afrikaners) in 1875 'to stand for our language, our nation and our land', produced a newspaper, *Die Afrikaanse Patriot*, written in Afrikaans rather than the Dutch currently in standard use, and published their own history book stressing the distinctiveness of the Afrikaner experience and the God-given destiny they possessed as a chosen people. This was the first time that such a view had been articulated. It was absent in the mid-nineteenth-century period of the Great Trek and the establishment of the Boer polities of the interior. Du Toit (1983) has argued that its emergence in the 1870s and 1880s was a conscious attempt by an elite class to stress social cohesion in the face of a process of industrialization and modernization over which it had little control.

In 1880 this movement found political expression in the foundation of the Afrikaner Bond, which contested seats in the Cape Legislative Assembly and established branches in other parts of South Africa. But in general the idea of Afrikaner unity attracted little support outside the western Cape. The governments of the Free State and the Transvaal saw no unity of interests with Afrikaners in the Cape, and by the 1890s the Afrikaner Bond was in parliamentary alliance with their arch-enemy, Cecil Rhodes.

However, in the western Cape the 'Patriot' movement did find other allies. Giliomee (1987) has shown how the wealthy wine and grain farmers of the region faced economic difficulties in the depression of the late 1870s and came to identify their interests in opposition to the English merchant and commercial classes. They demanded protective tariffs for their produce, state support for agriculture and adequate controls over labour. Not only did they support the Afrikaner Bond, they also backed local financial institutions in opposition to the London-based Standard Bank, and began to build a local capital base. By 1915, a strong Afrikaner nationalist bourgeoisie had emerged in the western Cape, consisting of farmers and professionals who were shareholders and directors of major financial institutions and intellectuals of the DRC and

Stellenbosch University. Afrikaner capital was used in 1915 to found the Nasionale Pers publishing house and the newspaper *De Burger* and to set up the large trust and insurance companies Santam and Sanlam in 1918.

In the Free State and South African (Transvaal) Republics, Afrikaners controlled the state. Attack from outside, such as the British annexation of the Transvaal in 1877 and the rebellion of 1881 which ousted them, mobilized support for the Republican cause by using Afrikaner symbols. But there were marked class divisions amongst Afrikaners in the north, and by the end of the nineteenth century poor bywoners had little in common with the wealthy farmers and commercial groups who controlled government (Giliomee 1989). During the South African War there was not universal support by Afrikaner speakers for the Boer cause. In particular, some bywoners and poor-white tenants had refused to join commandos led by the large landowners, and some even joined the British.

In the following decades Afrikaner class interests became even more divided, especially with the move of young men and women from the land into the towns. This gave some cause for alarm to Dutch Reformed ministers who saw the waning of church influence in the cities. In addition a small group of Afrikaner intellectuals and teachers, alienated by the anglicization of state education under Reconstruction, had formed separate schools, funded from Holland and independent of the state, advocating a distinctively Afrikaner 'Christian National' education.

In a conscious attempt to develop an Afrikaner ethnic identity in the face of industrialization and class division, these northern clerics and teachers mobilized support for the Afrikaans language and published newspapers and popular magazines such as *Die Huisgenoot* (Home Companion), stressing the common heritage of all Afrikaners, in an approach which mirrored the emphasis of anthropological studies on African 'traditional culture' of the time (Hofmeyr 1987). Furthermore, in 1918 a secret society, the Afrikaner Broederbond (Brotherhood), was established, dominated by Transvaal intellectuals and clergy, to mobilize political support. In 1929 it was instrumental in the founding of the Federasie van Afrikaanse Kultuurverenigings (Federation of Afrikaner Cultural Associations) to unify and disseminate a sense of separate Afrikaner identity.

Such developments certainly played an important role in mobilizing popular perceptions. But political mobilization of Afrikaner nationalism was not easy. Divisions of wealth and class persisted: bywoners and those Afrikaners who worked as unskilled labourers in the towns had little in common with the teachers and intellectuals of the Afrikaner cultural movement. However, during the First World War some of these divisions were breached. In 1914 a number of ex-Boer commando leaders rebelled against the Union government and marched to the defence of the Germans in South West Africa. Most of those who fought under them were poorer bywoners. The rebellion was put down and its leader executed but this act was identified by some Afrikaner intellectuals as the creation of a martyr.

Hertzog's National Party openly identified with the rebellion, opposed South African participation in 'England's war' and certainly benefited from heightened Afrikaner nationalist sentiment during the war years. But its main body of support were farmers who resented the dominance of mining and British capital interests in the state. Some poorer Afrikaners were also drawn in, but they still had little in common with landowners; and as they became increasingly urban-ized, their class interests led them to support the Labour Party. When in power after 1924, Hertzog gave support to official recognition of Afrikaans and introduced a new national flag to replace the Union Jack, but he placed greater emphasis on white national unity ('South Africa first') in contrast to imperial control, than to separatist Afrikaner ethnic mobilization.

Hertzog's alliance with Smuts in the Fusion government of 1934 marked a clear rejection of Afrikaner separatism and an alliance with British capital interests. It led to the breakaway of the Gesuiwerde Nasionale Party ('Purified' National Party) under Malan. Much of the ethnic symbolism built up by the Afrikaner Broederbond, the FAK and Nasionale Pers swung behind the new party. The western Cape farmer–intelligentsia alliance followed, but in the Free State and the Transvaal support for Malan was limited to some academics, teachers and clerics. Fusion threatened the status and position of these middle-class Afrikaners who had obtained greater access to govern-ment and administrative positions.

O'Meara (1983) argues that Fusion was a turning point in the political mobilization of Afrikaner ethnicity. After 1934 a conscious effort was made by the National Party to capture power by mobilizing Afrikaners across divisions of region and class. This was marked in three main ways. Firstly Afrikaner culture was further defined and propagated through the Afrikaner Broederbond, the FAK and Christian Nationalist education, stressing the need for *volkseenheid* (unity of the *volk*) in the face of political party divisions. The height of this development was the *Eeufees* celebration of the centenary of the Great Trek in 1938, which mobilized widespread popular interest and support in the symbols of an Afrikaner past, represented by the processions of ox wagons through the country and the founding of the Voortrekker Monument in Pretoria.

Secondly, a major attempt was made to win Afrikaner working-class support away from the English-dominated trade unions. These were attacked as 'foreign' and inimical to the interests of the *volk*. Attempts to establish alternative Afrikaner labour organizations were made which met with success where Afrikaner workers felt alienated from older craft unions, such as in the mines, but were not entirely successful elsewhere (O'Meara 1978). But although by no means all Afrikaner workers broke with the older unions, enough shifted loyalty from the Labour Party to the National Party to help it to win victory in 1948.

Thirdly, Afrikaner business and capital were actively encouraged and developed to meet the challenge of the overwhelming domination of these fields by English interests. Afrikaner capital had been largely based in the western Cape, but closer links between Sanlam and the Afrikaner Broederbond were now forged. In 1939, in the aftermath of the *Eeufees* euphoria, Sanlam underwrote the Reddingsdaadfons (Act of Rescue Fund) to support fledgling Afrikaner business interests. Stressing the need to counteract foreign-dominated capital and monopolies, which were stated to have caused proletarianization and class division amongst the *volk* and driven them into competition with black labour, Afrikaner business claimed by contrast to serve the entire Afrikaner community rather than merely enriching one sector of it. This *volkskapitalisme* marked a significant break with previous Afrikaner nationalist promotion of an idealized rural and pre-capitalist society. Afrikaner nationalism was now dealing head on with the realities of an industrialized society, although the importance of the earlier *volkskultuur* movement should not be under-estimated (Giliomee 1983).

It was only in the 1940s, however, that this process began to bear political fruit, largely aided by other events in South Africa and abroad. Smuts's immediate support of Britain at the outbreak of the Second World War in 1939 led to Hertzog's split from the Fusion alliance and his swift political demise. With him went supporters of the old Nationalist Party and those who could not follow Smuts's automatic acceptance of British interests. Malan's 'purified' National Party, which had benefited from its backing of the 1938 *eeufees*, was now poised to fill the gap as the true political home of Afrikaner nationalism. Pro-German sympathy was also expressed by some Afrikaner intellectuals and by the militant Ossewa Brandwag, which was founded as a cultural movement in 1938 but turned to active sabotage during the war. However, few Afrikaners actively supported such developments. The main thrust of support for Malan's National Party came not from the far-right organizations but from an alliance of voters who saw their own position threatened by the economic and social changes within South Africa of the war period and its aftermath.

In the 1943 elections, the National Party emerged as the official opposition, with forty-three seats against the government United and Labour Party coalition of 103 seats. Between then and 1948, a number of United Party and Labour Party voters shifted allegiance to the National Party. Paramount in this was the breakdown of segregation, marked by African urban influx, the relaxation of pass laws and the apparent inability of the state to deal with the rising tide of black protest. These were the products of the boost to secondary industry and urbanization provided by the war, as we have seen (pp. 61–4).

Although Malan had emphasized Afrikaner ethnic identity in the 1943 campaign, it was only after 1945 that the National Party began to stress racial issues and the need for a firm 'native policy'. Arguments for the need to protect distinct 'cultures' tended to dominate National Party thinking, owing as much to the views of the earlier segregationists as to overt notions of scientifically proven white race supremacy (Dubow 1992). In opposition to the government's Fagan Commission which recognized the inevitability of permanent African urbanization and the impracticability of enforcing the 1936 Land Act, the National Party's Sauer Report of 1946 thus recommended consolidation of the reserves, rigorous controls over African urban settlement, segregated facilities for coloureds and Indians and the abolition of the white representatives of Africans in Parliament. Coined as apartheid, this policy became the basis of Malan's campaign in the 1948 election.

Was apartheid simply segregation by another name? Some historians have argued that this essentially was so, although apartheid involved a more ruthless system of labour control. However, Wolpe (1972) has stressed the essential difference that by the 1940s the existing reserves were palpably incapable of maintaining a subsistence base for migrant workers, as earlier segregationist policy had envisaged. Apartheid thinkers thus planned to bolster the reserves with possibly more land, but also with manufacturing development closer to their boundaries.

But in the 1940s apartheid was not a single cohesive policy (Posel 1987). Although all of its supporters agreed on the need to maintain white supremacy by the total exclusion of Africans from political power, there were differences of opinion over other aspects of apartheid policy. Some intellectuals in the tradition of the Broederbond and the FAK advocated 'total segregation', with exclusion of Africans from 'white' towns and rural areas, their replacement by white immigrants and the consolidation of the reserves as self-contained economic units. Such a policy was clearly articulated by writers like W.M.M. Eiselen (1948), later to be the National Party Government Secretary of Native Affairs, and it also appealed to white workers. But businessmen and farmers needing continued access to black labour favoured a more 'practical apartheid' whereby labour mobility would be strictly controlled by the state, which would also permit supplies of African rural and urban workers to be obtained. The Sauer Report was sufficiently vague to accommodate both of these viewpoints and thus to attract a wide range of differing class interests. The ambiguity of apartheid was its electoral strength, although its differing interpretations were to emerge fully after 1948.

Apartheid thus provided the means of cementing the cross-class Afrikaner alliance which had been consciously forged in the preceding decades. It appealed to traditional National Party supporters: teachers, clerics, intellectuals and the large-scale farmers of the western Cape. But it also attracted significant new categories of voters. Many white workers, threatened by black urbanization during the Second World War and influenced by the FAK assault on the trade unions, deserted the Labour Party for Malan. Also Transvaal and Free State farmers were attracted to the prospect of cheap contract labour provision at a time when urbanization was making this difficult to obtain. They were also hostile to the Smuts government's price control policy which kept food cheaper for the towns. And small-scale Afrikaner traders and businessmen in Natal and the Transvaal welcomed the removal of Indian competition in more strictly segregated cities.

Smuts was somewhat complacent in the 1948 election campaign and vulnerable to Malan's accusations that he had placed British imperial interests above those of his own people and that under him segregation was collapsing. Nonetheless the results were close, and

93

Malan only obtained a slender majority. Apartheid had proved the basis of a rather fragile alliance behind this Afrikaner nationalist victory. Few of its opponents believed that such a government with such a policy could last for long.

SUGGESTIONS FOR FURTHER READING

Cell, J. 1982: *The highest stage of white supremacy: the origins of segregation in South Africa and the American South.* Cambridge: Cambridge University Press.

Marks, S. and Trapido, S. (eds) 1987: *The politics of race, class and nationalism in twentieth century South Africa.* London: Longman.

O'Meara, D. 1983: *Volkskapitalisme: class, capital and ideology in the development of Afrikaner nationalism 1934–1948.* Cambridge: Cambridge University Press; Johannesburg: Ravan.

5

The Heyday of Apartheid

The National Party retained control of government from 1948 into the 1990s and the history of South Africa in the second half of the twentieth century has been dominated by apartheid and the resistance it evoked. But apartheid has not been static or monolithic. Each decade, broadly speaking, was marked by differences in both the content and the implementation of the policy, as well as in ways of resistance. In this chapter we shall examine these changes in the heyday of apartheid between the 1950s and the 1976 Soweto revolt.

The 1950s: constructing apartheid

During the first decade of National Party government, a barrage of legislation codified and extended racial discrimination. As we have seen, much of this had precedents in segregationist laws and practices earlier in the century, but from the late 1940s the partial breakdown of segregation that had taken place during the years of the Second World War was reversed, and legislative discrimination was taken much further than before.

The cornerstone of apartheid was the division of all South Africans by race. Malan thus moved early to ensure the compartmentalization of the population. The prohibition of 'mixed marriages' (1949) and the Immorality Act (1950) extended the existing ban on sex between whites and Africans to prohibit all sexual contact between whites and other South Africans, including Indians and coloureds. Racial division in the future was the goal. And the Population Registration

95

Act of the same year enforced the classification of people into four racial categories: white, coloured, 'Asiatic' (Indian) and 'Native' (later 'Bantu' or African).

In subsequent years this rigid schema was extended to virtually every sphere of human activity. Residential segregation had existed in some parts of the country since the earlier part of the century, but the Group Areas Act (1950) extended the principle of separate racial residential areas on a comprehensive and compulsory basis (Mabin 1992). Its application was particularly felt in the cities. For instance, Indian traders were moved out of the centre of Pretoria and many coloured inhabitants of Cape Town suburbs were relocated in segregated areas despite local council objections. In 1954 the Natives Resettlement Act gave the state the power to override local municipalities and forcibly remove Africans to separate townships. Some of the first casualties were the African freehold areas of western Johannesburg such as Sophiatown, whose inhabitants were relocated to the new township at Soweto in 1955.

The Reservation of Separate Amenities Act (1953) enforced social segregation in all public amenities, such as transport, cinemas, restaurants and sports facilities. And educational apartheid was enforced in schools (1953), technical colleges (1955) and universities (1959). African schooling was still neither free nor compulsory, as it was for whites. Certainly educational provision for Africans before this period had been unequal and most government schools separated white and African pupils. However the Bantu Education Act (1953) brought all African schools under the control of the Department of Native Affairs, thus phasing out the independent missionary institutions which had previously led the field in African education. It also imposed a uniform curriculum which stressed separate 'Bantu culture' and deliberately prepared students for little more than manual labour. Verwoerd, then Minister of Native Affairs, commented that many previous educators of Africans 'misled them by showing them the green pastures of European society in which they are not allowed to graze' (Christie and Collins 1984: 173).

White political monopoly of power was further tightened in the early 1950s. The advisory Natives Representative Council, set up in 1936, was abolished. The Bantu Authorities Act (1951) replaced it with government-approved chiefs in the reserves but made no provision for the representation of Africans in the towns and 'white' rural areas. The system of white parliamentary representation for Indians, established in 1946, was also ended. The only remaining 'non-white' representation in Parliament was that of coloureds in the Cape. The National Party's electoral majority in 1948 was slender, and many marginal seats contained a number of coloured voters who had largely supported the United Party and who bitterly opposed the discrimination of the Population Registration, Group Areas and Separate Amenities legislation. In 1951 the government attempted to have them removed from the voters' roll. Such an action was only passed in Parliament with a bare majority and was declared unconstitutional by the Supreme Court. The government overcame this obstacle by rapidly appointing new senators to the upper house of Parliament who ensured the required two-thirds majority. Despite large-scale demonstrations of opposition by both coloureds and the white war veteran Torch Commando, in 1956 coloureds were registered on a separate roll and were restricted to electing four white representatives to Parliament (a system abolished in 1970). Total white monopoly of Parliamentary power was thus obtained.

Coloured disenfranchisement showed that the National Party was determined to go to great lengths to ensure its electoral survival, although it increased its majority in the 1953 election, coloured voters notwithstanding. Other legislation increased government control over its non-parliamentary opponents. The Suppression of Communism Act (1950) gave the Minister of Justice the power to ban any person or organization he viewed as 'communist', a broad definition which included almost all opposition to apartheid. Powers were developed to confine people to single magisterial districts and to silence their writings and speeches, a forerunner of the security legislation of later years. And the 1953 Criminal Law Amendment Act prescribed heavy penalties for civil disobedience, a response to the organized campaigns of the previous year (see p. 100).

All of these white supremacist actions met with the approval of every sector of the broad Afrikaner nationalist alliance. A more controversial plank of apartheid legislation in the 1950s related to control over black labour. African urbanization and assertive labour organization had been the main feature of the breakdown of segregation in the 1940s and Malan's call for restrictions on African workers and firmer influx control attracted much support in 1948. During the first few years of National Party power, a number of measures attempted to put such a policy into effect. Strikes by Africans were made illegal in 1953, and although black trade unions were not prohibited outright, employers were not obliged to negotiate with them and many of their leaders were banned under the

97

Suppression of Communism Act. Labour bureaux were established in 1951 under the control of the Native Affairs Department to co-ordinate the needs of employers in particular regions and the recruitment of Africans to work in the towns, ensuring that they did not leave 'white' rural areas until the needs of local farmers had been met. Illegal 'squatting' in urban areas was prohibited in 1951, and in 1952 the Orwellian-named Abolition of Passes and Coordination of Documents Act insisted that all Africans (including previously exempted women) carry a reference book to include an employer's signature renewed each month, authorization to be in a particular area and tax certificates. Under Section 10 of the 1955 Natives (Urban Areas) Amendment Act, rights of Africans to live in a town were confined to those who had been born there or had worked there for fifteen years or for ten years with a single employer. All others needed a permit to stay for longer than three days.

As Posel (1991) has argued, the 1955 Act demonstrated the triumph of a more pragmatic 'practical' approach to segregation over the 'total' segregation of men like Eiselen who argued that all African economic activity and labour should be concentrated in the reserves (see p. 93). The needs of agricultural and urban employers for a steady supply of African labour determined government policy. Thus Africans should be permitted to move to towns if they were genuinely seeking work and Section 10 recognized that 'detribalized' Africans had rights to urban residence whether or not they were employed there, thus providing a 'labour pool' for urban employers. Although pass laws were imposed, the labour bureaux were only partially successful in directing labour to where it was demanded. Employers circumvented many of these controls when it suited them to do so.

The needs of business explain why the segregation of the 1950s remained 'practical', and influx control was not strictly applied. Similarly, while the government still had a rather uncertain electoral majority and no central control over local municipalities, it was reluctant to attempt full-scale urban removals and the implementation of 'total' segregation. All this was to change in the subsequent decade.

In the 1958 election the National Party obtained almost twice as many seats as its opponents. Part of this increasing Parliamentary strength resulted from ploys such as the removal of the coloured franchise, the incorporation of the white (predominantly Nationalist) electorate of South West Africa and the redrawing of constituency boundaries to favour rural areas over United Party urban strongholds. But clearly apartheid genuinely appealed to an increasing majority of the white electorate. Why was this? Many Afrikaners approved the power exerted by a party in their name and the moves to break with Britain as marked by the abolition of rights of appeal to the Privy Council (1950) and assumption of control over the British naval base at Simonstown (1955). But it was clear by 1958 that the Nationalists was also attracting English-speaking voters away from the United Party. The latter saw its sixty-five seats held in 1948 whittled down to fifty-three, most of them going to the National Party.

Most whites supported the apparent limits to African urbanization imposed by the government and the suppression of resistance. But most significantly apartheid policies had not interrupted economic growth and white living standards increased steadily. Farmers benefited from increased produce prices and workers from racial job reservation. Although many English-speaking manufacturers and industrialists were alienated from Afrikaner nationalist politics, they were able to maintain and expand production and enjoyed tariff protection. Gold production expanded markedly with the exploitation of new fields in the Free State. Foreign investment, encouraged by cheap labour, furthered white prosperity, and there was little external criticism of apartheid policies. Only at the end of the decade did this change, with international condemnation and the flight of capital after the Sharpeville shootings. By then the National Party, now led by Hendrik Verwoerd, had acquired sufficient confidence and power to ride the storm.

The 1950s: defiance and the Freedom Charter

The 1950s saw an unprecedented upsurge of popular protest. In some ways this was a logical development from the trends seen in the 1940s, notably the doubling of the African urban population, employment in secondary industry and trade union organization. But it was given a new impetus by the imposition of apartheid laws and the social engineering of the Nationalist government. The intransigence of influx control (and especially the extension of passes to women), forced removals and the imposition of Bantu Education all led to resistance in the towns, drawing in both popular and middle classes. Despite the assault on union power, labour leaders organized protests around issues of low wages and price increases. Nor was resistance confined to the cities. Government intervention in reserve agriculture and the unpopularity of measures carried out by chiefs appointed under the Bantu Authorities Act led to a number of rural protest movements. And the international context of decolonization elsewhere in Africa gave black political leaders hope that the construction of apartheid was a temporary aberration soon to be swept away in the wake of popular support for African nationalism.

Many of the tactics employed in this resistance, such as boycotts, stayaways, strikes and civil disobedience, were those advocated in the African National Congress's (ANC's) Programme of Action of 1949 (see p. 87). In 1952 the ANC and the Communist Party jointly launched the Defiance Campaign to protest against the government's new discriminatory legislation, with the aim of mobilizing widespread defiance of unjust laws such as curfews, pass laws and segregation of amenities. Over 8,000 people were arrested for defiance actions, mainly in the eastern Cape and on the Rand, and during the period of 1951–3 ANC membership grew dramatically from 7,000 to 100,000 (Lodge 1987: 310). Albert Lutuli, elected ANC President in late 1952, supported the principle of mass action in a clear break from the more conservative techniques of his predecessors. The Defiance Campaign was broken by the banning and imprisonment of many of its organizers, by legislation forbidding civil disobedience (the Criminal Law Amendment Act of 1953) and by outbreaks of violence in Port Elizabeth and East London. But the impetus for mass campaigns was clearly established.

The relocation of Sophiatown, which began in 1953, was resisted by local residents. Property owners refused to sign away their rights, and, together with other tenants who would not move voluntarily, had to be forcibly relocated by the police. In 1954 the ANC called for a boycott of the new Bantu Education schools, an action which achieved considerable success initially on the Rand and in the eastern Cape. However, ANC promises of alternative informal education were only partially fulfilled and when the government threatened to blacklist teachers who supported the boycott and to permanently deny education to any children not enrolled by April of the academic year, opposition to Bantu Education collapsed.

More sustained campaigns were carried out from 1952 by women against the carrying of passes. The Federation of South African Women, founded in 1954, linked to the ANC but drawing on other liberal supporters, coordinated campaigns of non-registration, pass burning and petitioning, culminating in 1956 in a mass demonstration of 26,000 women from throughout the country at the Union Buildings in Pretoria. This opposition certainly slowed down state action in extending passes to African women, but it failed to prevent it. The government began issuing passes to women in remoter rural areas, and then to the most vulnerable urban workers, such as domestic workers and nurses, the latter being threatened with dismissal if they refused to comply.

By 1959, the anti-pass campaign was over. Women's protest turned instead to focus on police raids against shebeens, which threatened the dependence of many township women on informal beer-brewing (see p. 62). In 1959 women in the shanty settlement of Cato Manor near Durban and in other parts of Natal picketed municipal beerhalls and in some cases attacked them and destroyed brewing equipment. Police broke up the protestors, but a boycott of beerhalls followed.

Protest by women was an important part of popular mobilization in the 1950s, but this was not so much a feminist attempt to overthrow the existing social order as opposition to state interference in the established rights and status of women. Indeed, Lodge has described some of the goals of the campaigns as 'highly conservative . . . though no less justifiable for that' (1983: 151).

Other community-based actions emerged in the late 1950s. In 1957 buses were boycotted in the Rand township of Alexandra in campaigns against increased fares that invoked memories of the campaigns of 1944 (see pp. 63–4). In the wake of this, union leaders in the newly formed South African Council of Trade Unions convinced the ANC of the need for a wider campaign around economic issues. The £1-a-day campaign of 1957–8 called for a minimum wage and better working conditions, but its tactics of stayaway, combined in 1958 with protest against the white election of that year, met with only limited success. Police were readily able to identify those who remained at home, and dismissals for absenteeism from work took place. Moreover, as Feit has pointed out, the campaign was untimely. Wage levels were not noticeably lower than usual, and a number of urban workers were earning more than £1 a day (1967: 17). And the white election was of less immediate concern than day-to-day issues in the townships. Campaigns of this kind were difficult to sustain. Specific and limited targets were better supported.

Perhaps the most successful mass campaigns of the decade took place not in the towns but in the countryside. Rural conflicts around issues of impoverishment and state intervention were not new, but they rose to new heights in the late 1940s and the 1950s (Chaskalson 1988). Attempts by the government to improve reserve agriculture, by 'betterment' schemes of cattle culling and limitations on grazing, were

101

fiercely resisted at a time when the sole means of survival for many homesteads was access to such land and stock. Moreover the Bantu Authorities Act made local chiefs responsible for these measures, as well as for tax collection. By implementing state policies many of them forfeited local recognition of their powers, and their appointment by the government further undermined their authority in such situations.

Attacks on local chiefs took place in the northern Transvaal (Soutpansberg and Sekhukhuneland) in the 1940s and again in 1956. In Witzieshoek, in the northern Free State, cattle were seized by reserve inhabitants before they could be culled, fences were torn down and clashes with the police took place. In Zeerust in the western Transvaal in 1957 chiefs appointed by the Native Affairs Department were deposed, and similar actions took place in both Natal and the Transkei. In Pondoland in 1960 a major revolt took place against government chiefs and agents. Many of these uprisings used traditional symbols and appeals. But they were by no means all 'backward-looking' peasant revolts. Links were made with urban protests especially in regions where migrants brought news of other campaigns, such as those against Bantu Education or passes for women. But in general, although they did succeed in stalling state interventions, rural protest movements remained parochial in impact (Lodge 1983).

Indeed all the popular struggles of the 1950s failed to fully realize their potential in challenging the state. One of the reasons for this, much debated by historians, was the nature of the relationship between mass mobilization and the leadership of the national organizations, in particular the ANC. Was the ANC now converted from the elitist and essentially conservative body of the 1930s to a new and mass-based movement with more radical goals and heightened impact? Some writers have argued that this was indeed the case, either in co-ordination with the labour movement as the political base for a new class consciousness heralded by the 1946 mine workers' strike (O'Meara 1976), or in the broader sense that the ANC acted as the vanguard party planning and sustaining all popular movements of the decade (Pampallis 1991: 191–211).

But other historians have pointed out the limitations of these arguments. Links with trade union branches were made, but the middle-class leaders of the ANC were still uneasy in a proletarian alliance and local campaigns often went beyond the calls of ANC leadership or else were not supported at all by the organization

(Lambert 1981; Fine and Davis 1991). Broader populist causes rather than class-conscious action dominated ANC activities. Feit (1971) goes further, arguing that ANC leadership was detached from any popular base, that communication and co-ordination of actions were at best patchy and that many campaigns failed as a result.

For instance in Sophiatown the ANC appeared more concerned with the rights of property owners than with the plight of the larger number of tenants or the wider issue of forced removals, and it was divided over how far to resist legal eviction orders. Leaders were also split over how far to take the school boycott and were often unaware of the extent of local community support. During the Alexandra bus boycott, Congress's acceptance of the compromise by which employers could obtain transport rebates to pass on to their employees rather than lowering fares for all was rejected by many in the community as a sell-out. And only gradually did the urban leaders of the ANC come to recognize the importance of the rural areas. Not until the uprisings in Pondoland in 1960 was the full potential of rural mobilization accepted (Bundy 1987a). In general, the 1950s seems to have been a decade of heightened defiance but also of lost opportunities.

Some of these debates show as much about the political sympathies and priorities of the writers in later years as they do about the nature of political mobilization in the 1950s. Clearly the ANC failed to mobilize and co-ordinate widespread unified protest, as much because of its limited financial and administrative resources and heightened state repression as because of the conscious alienation of its leaders from popular or working class interests. Lodge, however, has pointed out that the situation was more complex (1987). ANC leaders were not merely 'middle-class' professionals alienated from popular issues. With the segregationist thrust of the 1950s, African experiences were widely felt across class lines, and issues such as Bantu Education or passes for women affected everyone.

Case studies have shown that particular local circumstances need to be considered when assessing the effectiveness of campaigns and of national leadership. Thus in East London, active support was obtained for the Defiance Campaign by the dynamic local Youth League, which also drew in migrants from the surrounding Ciskei reserve, but the lack of a large urban proletariat led to emphasis on communal rather than class issues in later years (Lodge 1987). By contrast unionized textile workers in Benoni organized a number of strikes and stoppages; but organizers had difficulty in linking these up

103

with the interests of the unemployed who were more concerned with general survival than specific issues and mobilized around gangs split on ethnic lines rather than labour or national organizations (Bonner and Lambert 1987). In Brakpan stronger cross-class unity took place around issues of Bantu Education, curfews and pass laws, but these tended to be focused around locally elected councillors rather than national leaders who failed to realize the extent of local feeling (Sapire 1989a).

The opposition movements not only faced difficulties of tactics and popular mobilization. They were also increasingly divided in terms of ideology. Some of these divisions were rooted in the differing organizations of the 1940s. For instance the Non-European Unity Movement stressed the importance of tactics of boycott and non-collaboration, which had an impact on some of the defiance campaigns, particularly in the rejection of Bantu Education schools. But its theoretical focus on the interests of the working class and its refusal to recognize race as a valid category of political organization alienated it from the ANC which it believed advocated 'pro-capitalist, anti-working class ... bourgeois social democracy'. The Unity Movement's strength lay in the western Cape, but although it was strong on theory, advocating a strongly Trotskyist line, it never mustered the degree of numerical active support obtained by the ANC (Nasson 1990).

But there were also divisions within the ANC. The crucial issue was whether Congress should link up with other organizations opposing apartheid, such as the radical white Congress of Democrats, or whether it should follow a strictly Africanist course, rejecting association with all non-African associations ranging in political terms from the moderate Liberal Party to the Communist Party. Under Lutuli the former policy triumphed. In the aftermath of the Defiance Campaign, and in the face of government banning of civil disobedience, plans were made to bring together opponents of apartheid in the hope that sheer numbers and force of moral argument would lead to its overthrow.

It was also felt necessary to demonstrate multiracial unity to counter charges made by the state that racial segregation was natural and desired by all. The example it frequently gave of the dangers of inter-racial contact was the violent conflicts between Africans and Indians that took place in Durban in 1949, in which 142 people were killed, over a thousand injured and many trading stores and houses looted. In this case ethnic tension had been heightened by specific

104

local circumstances (Webster 1977). Africans were denied trading licences and the right to own freehold property, both of which were obtainable by Indians. Indian monopoly over commerce, transport and property ownership (many African tenants had Indian landlords) gave an ethnic focus to economic grievances at a time of increasing prices. Moreover, the verbal assault of the state on Indians, including the argument that they had no place in South Africa and should be returned to India, encouraged some Africans in the belief that the government would approve of attacks on their property.

The 1949 Durban riots, coming at the very start of the period of National Party government, were an important weapon in claims that South Africans of different ethnicity could never co-exist peacefully. It was thus crucial for those opposing apartheid legislation to demonstrate that this was not the case.

In 1953 the ANC made links with the Congress of Democrats, the Indian Congress movement and the South African Coloured People's Organisation (the successor to the APO) in order to launch a National Congress of the People. Local committees collected lists of grievances and demands, which were then drafted by a central committee into the 'Freedom Charter'. This was accepted unanimously by the 2,844 delegates who gathered at Kliptown near Johannesburg in June 1955, and was later endorsed by all member organizations and by the South African Communist Party.

The government was unable to prevent such a gathering since the Congress of the People did not contravene existing laws. However, in the following year 156 of its leaders were arrested on charges of treason and 'conspiracy to overthrow the state' and the Congress was labelled a Communist movement. After lengthy proceedings, the state's case was overturned by the Supreme Court in 1961, an action which played an important part in the government's determination to rule without legal restraint (see p. 108). But the Treason Trial served to publicize the cause of the 'Charterists' more widely, both at home and abroad.

Charterism became the foundation of ANC ideology and the Freedom Charter remained a benchmark of opposition to apartheid into the 1990s. There has therefore been much debate about its meaning. Its clauses stressed that

South Africa belongs to all who live in it, black and white, and no government can justly claim authority unless it is based on

105

the will of the people . . . the rights of the people shall be the same regardless of race, colour or sex

and it demanded that 'all apartheid laws and practices shall be set aside'. It called for equal access to health, education and legal rights. Its vision of a future South Africa was thus strongly democratic and multiracial (Williams 1988). But its commitment to meaningful social and economic transformation was less clear. Trade unionists were dissatisfied with its lack of reference to worker control or the right to strike. It called for 'public ownership of mines and banks' and the re-division of land 'amongst those who work it', but it fell short of a clear commitment to socialism. It was adopted by the Communist Party, which by the late 1950s had come to accept that a national-democratic stage of revolution had to precede socialist transformation (Hudson 1988). This was sufficient to ensure objection to the Charter by the Liberal Party which steadfastly opposed any links with a radical strategy. But on the other hand the Charter has been rejected by other left-wing organizations for its lack of radicalism.

But the main opposition to the Freedom Charter among the nationalist organizations in the 1950s came from the Africanists. Charterism rejected Lembede's belief that only Africans owned South Africa (see p. 86). After his death in 1947, Africanist ideas were taken up by other younger members of the ANC, especially in the Orlando branch under Potlako Leballo. Their publication, *The Africanist*, stressed the need for closer links with mass protests, and it rejected Congress alliances with organizations such as the Indian Congress and the Communist Party. It viewed the Freedom Charter as a 'political bluff'. In 1958 tensions between Africanists and Charterists within the ANC reached a head, and after failing to capture control of the Transvaal executive a number of Africanists formed a new organization, the Pan Africanist Congress (PAC), in 1959 under the presidency of Robert Sobukwe, with the slogan of 'Africa for the Africans'.

Africanism was aided by a number of factors. It reflected the impatience of a younger generation with the liberal style of such men as Lutuli. It was part of a wider African assertiveness in this period, marked locally by increased support for the African Independent churches and more widely by the strength of African nationalism elsewhere, as shown by the 1958 Accra conference. Moreover Africanists could point to the failure of the Charterists in achieving

106

any success at halting the tide of discrimination, let alone driving it back (Gerhart 1978).

PAC membership numbers were lower than those of the ANC, but it captured the sense of township frustration in the late 1950s, especially on the Rand but also in the western Cape where influx control was stringently applied and Section 10 rights strictly limited. The PAC was determined to capitalize on this advantage. In December 1959 the ANC announced a series of single day anti-pass marches. By contrast the PAC called for a more sustained campaign, involving refusal to carry passes and mass presentation at police stations to demand arrest. This was the background to the peaceful march to the police station at Sharpeville in March 1960. Constables alarmed by the size of the crowd panicked and fired. Sixty-nine people died, many shot in the back, and 180 were wounded. A large crowd also marched from the Langa township into central Cape Town, although it disbanded without bloodshed when its leader Philip Kgosana was falsely promised an interview with the Minister of Justice.

The Sharpeville shootings marked a dramatic turning-point in South Africa's history. Strikes and stayaways followed throughout the country and the government declared a State of Emergency, detaining ANC and PAC leaders and then banning both organizations. Sharpeville revealed the failure of non-violent resistance and forced a new approach from opponents of apartheid. And internationally the 1960 shootings had a major effect. Currency controls were introduced in an attempt to stem the flight of capital. Serious calls for economic sanctions against South Africa were made at the United Nations, although they were vetoed by Britain and the United States who continued high levels of investment in South Africa throughout the 1960s and 1970s.

Just one month before the Sharpeville shootings, the British Prime Minister, Harold Macmillan, had addressed the South African Parliament in Cape Town. Following a tour of Africa during which he had been impressed by the power of African nationalism, he warned that the 'winds of change' were sweeping through the continent, and that Verwoerd's apartheid policies would find no support from a Britain now committed to rapid decolonization. Verwoerd had already mooted the possibility of forming a republic independent of the Commonwealth. Later that year, following heightened criticism of his policies at the Commonwealth conference, Verwoerd withdrew South Africa from the organization. The path was set for increasing isolation from the political trends elsewhere in Africa and the world at large in the decades ahead.

State control and separate development: apartheid's 'second phase'

After the steady consolidation of National Party electoral power in the 1950s, the following years saw the entrenchment of state control and new methods of dealing with opposition. The 1960s have therefore been labelled the years of apartheid's second phase (Posel 1991).

International condemnation after Sharpeville was firmly rejected by Verwoerd, who turned his back on the 'winds of change' sweeping Africa. The police force was increased in size and the new recruits were almost entirely Afrikaners. In the face of determined opposition campaigns, the General Law Amendment Act (1963) gave police powers of detention without charge and of solitary confinement. The banning of the ANC and PAC was accompanied by increasing numbers of such detentions and bannings of individuals. These tactics were to be the mainstay of internal repression into the 1990s. As Wolpe (1988: 88–9) has pointed out, after Sharpeville wide-ranging arbitrary powers provided a new means of state control, circumventing judicial intervention. Repetition of the state's defeat in the Treason Trial was not to be permitted.

The early 1960s also saw a more determined application of African urban influx control. A change of policy from that of the 1950s now led to attempts to remove rights of urban residence from all Africans, including those previously accepted under Section 10 of the Natives (Urban Areas) Amendment Act of 1955 (Posel 1991). This was caused by several factors. The state was alarmed by the increase in urban protest which had reached a climax at Sharpeville. Attempts to curb the urban radicalism of the 1940s had clearly failed. Moreover local municipalities were either unwilling or unable to control urban influx, as shown by the Durban Council's admission during the Cato Manor upheavals of 1959 that it 'has been defeated . . . and cannot restore its authority without the fullest co-operation and most active assistance of the government' (Posel 1991: 237).

New voices were heard within the Afrikaner nationalist alliance. The Broederbond had actively campaigned for Verwoerd's succession to the Party leadership in 1958, and now held a much stronger position behind the scenes of decision making. Its members, already influential in many branches of the government, infiltrated the Native

108

(renamed Bantu) Affairs Department (BAD) and also won over the South African Agricultural Union by advocating the limitation of urban African workers. In this context the stricter segregationist ideals of the Broederbond overrode the 'practical' segregation of the 1950s. In the months after Sharpeville, the BAD drafted a bill advocating the ending of Section 10 rights, the fixing of regional labour quotas by the Department with no reference to employers, and the preference to be given to industries willing to relocate to areas near the reserves.

The bill was fiercely opposed by commercial and industrial employers, including the Afrikaanse Handelsinstituut, and the government backed down. However, in the 1960s efforts were made by the state to enforce influx control more strictly, and although Section 10 remained on the statute books, the rights of urban Africans were increasingly restricted. For instance in 1964 the Bantu Labour Act prohibited Africans from seeking work in towns or employers from taking them on unless they were channelled through the state labour bureaux. Urban housing construction for black families almost came to a halt, thus causing major shortages. And in 1968 Africans were forbidden from holding freehold property in townships but were obliged to become tenants in council-owned housing.

The opposition of urban employers to total urban influx control by the state raises the question of the relationship between apartheid policy and capitalist interests. Certainly in a broad sense apartheid did not limit economic – particularly manufacturing – growth in the 1960s. Despite loss of foreign investor confidence after Sharpeville, local capital filled the gap, and the comparative calm of the 1960s saw an economic boom with increased foreign trade and industrial growth, although black wages remained low and racial disparities of wealth increased still further. This has led many to argue that apartheid, like segregation before it, favoured capitalist growth, particularly since it ensured a continued supply of cheap labour. But as Posel has argued, 'apartheid neither automatically nor uniformly promoted capitalist interest' (1984: 2). Manufacturers needed a skilled and permanent labour force and opposed stricter influx controls and total segregation. In the 1970s the disjuncture between capitalist needs and apartheid ideology grew wider (see pp. 121–2).

The tightening of influx control and attempts to revoke Section 10 rights were part of a broader plan of political and social engineering which was implemented under Verwoerd and his successors. This was 'Separate Development', a policy by which the reserves served a political rather than a purely economic purpose, as Bantustans to which African political rights were confined.

The Bantustan strategy was only gradually developed. The 1951 Bantu Authorities Act had attempted to co-opt a local elite with limited administrative powers. The Tomlinson Commission, set up to enquire into the economic viability of the reserves as self-contained units on the strict segregationist model, reported in 1955 that this could only be achieved with massive state funding, a commitment which Verwoerd refused to accept. But increasing political pressure from Africans gave strength to the idea of locating African political rights away from the urban centres to the peripheries, thus counteracting the nationalist goals of organizations such as the ANC and PAC. The 1959 Promotion of Bantu Self-Government Act set up eight (later extended to ten) distinct 'Bantu Homelands' out of the existing reserves, each with a degree of self-government. Not only did this greatly extend the powers of co-opted local chiefs, but it established the principle of ethnicity as the basis of the homelands. Africans were divided up into distinct 'nations' based on their 'historic

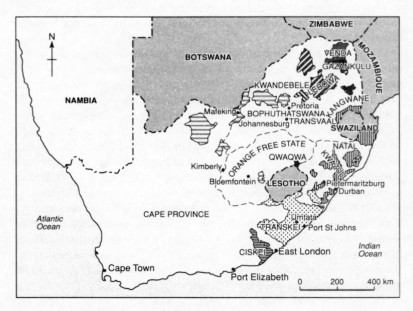

Map 4 The Bantustans (Homelands) *Source*: J. Omer-Cooper, 1987: *History of Southern Africa*, London: James Currey, 214.

110

homelands'. Ethnic homeland loyalty was to replace national political aspirations in a move which the state hoped would defuse calls for the moral necessity of African self-government within South Africa itself. In 1963 the Transkei Constitution Act set up the first homeland legislative assembly, significantly in the area most recently convulsed by rebellion and one where Pretoria was anxious to rid itself of the responsibility of keeping control. In 1970 homeland citizenship was imposed on all Africans throughout South Africa, and self-government was given to the other homelands in 1971. Nominal independence was given the Transkei in 1976, followed by Bophuthatswana (1977), Venda (1979) and Ciskei (1981). By this process, citizens of the 'independent' homelands lost their South African nationality, although the homelands were not recognized as independent by any other country.

Clearly the political significance of separate development was more important than the economic motives of earlier segregationist policies. Economic self-sufficiency was never a viable or desired option. Verwoerd refused to permit industries to be developed within the reserves which would risk the emergence of a stable and politically dangerous proletariat. Instead, he encouraged them to set up on the borders of the homelands where they were removed from the urban centres of South Africa but had access to cheap migrant labour. The focus of separate development was 'political independence with economic interdependence' (Giliomee 1985).

The homelands policy had fundamental implications for modern South Africa. Firstly it led to the forced relocation of Africans on an unprecedented scale. The Group Areas Act produced urban removals and dispossession. Separate Development extended this by removing into the homelands the sizeable number of African tenants, free-holders and squatters who were still in 'white' rural areas. Many of them were no longer required on farms which had mechanized. Thus the process begun in 1913 was brought to its logical conclusion. Between 1960 and 1983, an estimated 3.5 million people were relocated under Group Areas and Separate Development legislation (Platzky and Walker 1985: 10). During the 1960s the population of the Bantustans rose by 70 per cent, while those of African townships actually fell (Lodge 1983: 321). Forced removals on such a massive scale were the crudest sign of state power over black lives. In most cases those relocated to homelands were consigned to barren areas far removed from employment or adequate resources. Critics of apartheid labelled such actions as tantamount to genocide.

111

Secondly, Separate Development stimulated and entrenched ethnic divisions by its attempts to 'retribalize African consciousness' (Molteno 1977: 23). To succeed, such a policy had to be built on existing perceptions and ethnic division could not be simply imposed from above. Certainly differing historical experiences and traditions existed. Yet as recent work has shown, tribal identity was not a fixed constant (Vail 1989). The experience of conquest, proletarianization and social dislocation shattered pre-colonial polities and the identities that came with them. Tribalism was remoulded and consciously shaped by new forces. The linguistic and cultural tribal divisions of modern South Africa were in large part defined by outsiders in the first few decades of the twentieth century. Missionaries established written norms for Bantu languages, usually based on particular dialects of regions in which their printing presses were located. Anthropologists and historians identified distinct tribal cultures and traditions in the model of European ethnology and national histories. In the circumstances of the 1920s and 1930s these notions found fertile ground among 'native' administrators concerned to bolster 'traditional culture' and to overcome class divisions (see pp. 76–8). They also appealed to local chiefs as a means of bolstering their position and to some middle-class African teachers and intellectuals who adopted the role of interpreters of 'tribal tradition'. This combination of administrative and local interests in the making of new tribal identities was most apparent in Natal where Zulu ethnicity was strengthened by an alliance of state, landowners and the black middle class (see p. 82). Tribal identity was given further emphasis by the experience of migrant workers whose ethnic roots were reinforced by their dependence on the reserves and by competition in the workplace. Even those imbued with class or wider national political consciousness meshed these identities with a degree of ethnic particularism (Beinart 1987).

Thus the concept of separate ethnic identity drew on a lengthy process of created tribalism. In some cases such as Zululand or the Transkei, the argument that the Bantustans were the rightful historic home of a particular ethnic group coincided with common perceptions. Elsewhere this was not so. Bophuthatswana, for instance, was a cobbled together collection of seven widely scattered areas of land, all of them undesirable for commercial agriculture. Its historical heritage was tenuous to say the least. And even the most ardent advocate of tribalism could not explain the existence of two distinct Xhosa homelands, the Ciskei and the Transkei.

Nonetheless a sense of homeland identity did take root, even in Bophuthatswana. This was the result of the third lasting legacy of Separate Development in modern South Africa, the creation of new classes in the homelands. In a continuation of the policy of co-opting local chiefs, the Bantustan strategy gave Bantustan administrators considerable wealth, patronage and power. This served the dual purpose of creating local representatives of the state with vested interests to control popular opposition of the kind which had emerged in the 1950s, and of hopefully defusing critics by devolving political power to African authorities. This is not to say that homeland leaders were all absolute puppets of Pretoria. Matanzima, ruler of the Transkei, was critical of Bantu Education and of the way in which forced removals dumped people into his territory, but his general support of Separate Development earned him financial and military backing from the South African government, and also attracted allegiance from the educated elite in the rapidly growing homeland bureaucracy (Southall 1982).

In addition to bureaucrats and politicians, a class of African traders and entrepreneurs also benefited from the Bantustan strategy. As Molteno (1977) has pointed out, whereas in the early part of the century the government aimed to undermine an African middle class, by the 1960s it was trying to create one, albeit dependent on South African capital and support as a means of linking it to apartheid structures and policies. Loans and grants set up local capitalists, and many also benefited from the departure of white traders from the homelands, giving the 'new African trading class a stake in the political order' (Stadler 1987: 139).

Separate development was thus a bold attempt to break down a broad African nationalism and to replace it with tribal identities, led by new classes of collaborators. It could only be achieved with systematic and ruthless state intervention. How far it succeeded in achieving its goal remained to be seen.

After Sharpeville: decade of quietude?

In comparison with the resistance of the 1950s and with the upheavals of the 1970s and 1980s, the 1960s appears to have been a decade in which protest against apartheid was relatively muted. The banning of resistance organizations, increased police powers of detention and heightened state control over publications, broadcasting and all forms of dissent were clear reasons for this. And the ruthless policy of forced removals weakened the potential for urban resistance, while the Bantustans provided one outlet for the previously frustrated careers of the African middle class.

Another factor which may explain the relative quiescence of the 1960s was economic. Despite the crisis of investor confidence immediately after Sharpeville, the decade was one of unprecedented economic growth for South Africa. The gross national product grew at over 5 per cent per annum, and average real wages increased at a steady level (Terreblanche and Nattrass 1990: 14). Certainly the benefits of this were limited primarily to the white population, and the racial disparities of wealth were enormous. Yet in contrast to the periods of labour resistance and protest in the post-war years, or those that were to come in the 1970s and 1980s, levels of black unemployment in the 1960s were relatively low. Overall, it appears that less than 10 per cent of the economically active population as a whole were unemployed during the 1960s. The figure was to rise to 20 per cent and above in the subsequent decades (Wilson and Ramphele 1989: 84–5). Relative economic stability, as well as state oppression, explains the comparative lack of oppositional protest during the 1960s.

However, the lack of overt resistance on the scale of previous years should not be seen as a sign of acquiescence. Less visible developments were taking place which provided a crucial background to the renewal of overt protest in subsequent years.

The banning of the ANC and the PAC after Sharpeville did not lead to their eclipse, but to a necessary change of strategy. Attempts to organize stayaways and strikes were weakened by the difficulties of underground organization. At the end of 1961 armed struggle was therefore proposed as an alternative tactic. Some ANC leaders, including Mandela, Sisulu and other ex-Youth League organizers, were determined that direct action should begin. Umkhonto we Sizwe (Spear of the Nation) was founded as an underground guerrilla army, and a number of sabotage attacks on power stations and government installations were made over the next three years. At the same time a small group of predominantly white radicals known as the National Committee of Liberation (later renamed the African Resistance Movement) planned a sabotage campaign and planted bombs in Cape Town and Johannesburg. And in the western Cape, where PAC support was strong, an underground movement known as Poqo

('Pure' or 'Alone' in Xhosa) emerged, with rather indiscriminate plans to provoke a general uprising by killing police, suspected informers and government agents as well as whites. Some attacks of this kind occurred in Langa township near Cape Town, and a short-lived uprising took place in the rural town of Paarl in November 1962. Poqo also worked amongst peasants in the Transkei where it acquired a quasi-millenarian character, and some attacks on collaborating chiefs took place.

Davis and Fine (1985) have stressed that the move to armed struggle was a decision of leaders of the nationalist movements but had in fact already been effected by popular actions. Armed resistance had taken place prior to 1961–2, as in Pondoland in 1960. Hopes of mobilizing a general uprising were not fulfilled. And all of the early underground movements were broken by police arrests. Aided by the British colonial police in Basutoland who seized membership lists from the PAC office in Maseru, many PAC activists in South Africa were detained in early 1963. In July of that year the headquarters of Umkhonto at Rivonia were raided, and its leaders captured and sentenced to life imprisonment on Robben Island. The African Resistance Movement was infiltrated and broken up. Although the Non-European Unity Movement was not itself banned, it was unable to fill the vacuum created by the repression of the other liberation organizations and was split by ideological division, with some of its members leaving South Africa and others being arrested on charges of sabotage (Davies et al. 1988: 313). By 1964 leaders of the resistance movements were either in prison or had escaped to exile abroad.

Both the ANC and the PAC faced major difficulties as exiled organizations in the 1960s. Although they found bases in friendly countries, the ANC in Zambia and the PAC first in Lesotho and then in Tanzania, they were isolated from developments within South Africa. It was difficult to mount infiltration campaigns into the country, given its terrain, the strength of the defence forces and the ring of surrounding countries allied to Pretoria. Attempts at coordinated campaigns were made between ANC cadres and Zimbabwean guerrillas and by the PAC in Swaziland, but they failed to penetrate South Africa. Only with the collapse of white rule in Angola (1974), Mozambique (1975) and Zimbabwe (1979) did greater opportunities for guerrilla action emerge. Many of the rank and file members of the organizations were frustrated by inactivity in isolated and poorly equipped training camps.

Ideological and personal rifts also weakened both bodies, especially the PAC whose goal of Africanist struggle was difficult to maintain out of its South African context. The ANC was in general more successful in obtaining international support, although it was still treated warily by the Western powers. Both the PAC and the ANC survived in early exile, ready to take a more active role in the later 1970s and 1980s, but during the 1960s and early 1970s their influence within South Africa was much reduced. The expectations of mass confrontation raised in the early 1960s did not materialize.

What did emerge in the later 1960s was the powerful new ideology of Black Consciousness. Although at this stage Black Consciousness was more of a philosophical movement than an active political programme, it did fill some of the vacuum created by the banning of the nationalist organizations.

Black Consciousness ideas originated amongst university students. The creation of new segregated universities led to a marked increase in the number of African students after 1958. Some were particularly influenced by American developments in black theology, and formed the University Christian Movement. There was growing awareness of the ideas of black separatism which took institutional form. Many African students were frustrated by white domination of the National Union of South African Students, and in 1969 they split away to establish the all-black South African Students' Organisation (SASO), under the presidency of a student from the segregated medical school at the University of Natal, Steve Biko.

Although SASO was a student organization its members encouraged blacks in other contexts to break away from white-dominated liberal organizations. The Black Communities Project was formed to encourage and support black self-help schemes. In 1971 representatives of these bodies set up the Black People's Convention (BPC) to provide a political body organized along Black Consciousness principles. But this failed to gain a large membership. It was limited by inadequate funding and state repression and also by the reluctance of many to be involved with an overtly political movement, thus 'vindicating the view held by Steve Biko and others that black people had first to be "liberated from fear" ' (Buthelezi 1991: 126).

It was on such psychological grounds that Black Consciousness explained the failure of ANC and PAC tactics. Black inferiority, induced by years of oppression and of white liberal paternalism, prevented effective organization and resistance. Blacks therefore needed to acquire a social identity of their own. As Biko stated, 'what

Black Consciousness seeks to do is to produce . . . real black people who do not regard themselves as appendages to white society' (1978: 51). Black Consciousness was thus an attitude of mind, a conscientization necessary for political activism to succeed. Although Black Consciousness advocators included supporters of both the ANC and the PAC, their political and economic programme was vague. They advanced black communalism, said to be rooted in indigenous culture and based on the principle of sharing of wealth, although they also accepted the need for private property. Only after the banning of Black Consciousness organizations in 1977 did its leaders advocate a more radical socialist programme (Leatt et al. 1986: 105–19).

Black Consciousness drew on a number of distinct traditions. In a broad sense its emphasis on black pride and self-assertion was modelled on similar developments in the United States and the experience of the African diaspora, as well as on the ideas of such writers as Fanon and Senghor. The American Civil Rights Movement of the 1960s gave a particularly strong impetus to increasing black assertiveness. In the South African context Black Consciousness followed some of the arguments of the Africanist and PAC traditions by stressing that South Africa belonged to its black people alone and by its rejection of liberalism and white-dominated organizations. However, Biko's definition of black was more one of attitude than of ethnicity. It included all of those oppressed by apartheid, thus extending the term to bring in 'coloured' and Indian South Africans, but excluded those whose collaboration with apartheid structures such as the police or Bantustan administrations still defined them as 'non-whites'. White opponents of apartheid had no place in Black Consciousness organizations, but should rather conscientize their 'racist brethren' (Halisi 1991).

Black Consciousness also developed in the context of the international student revolt of the late 1960s, and was a distinctly generational and intellectual movement which did not penetrate far into working class or peasant communities. The ANC viewed it as a useful means of arousing self-awareness but limited in its abilities to effect political action. Others rejected its philosophy. The Unity Movement disapproved of the primacy that it gave to race over class and the ineffectiveness of 'self-help' organizations to change the fundamental structure of society (Alexander 1991).

The state initially believed that Black Consciousness could further its plans of separate development but soon learnt otherwise. Biko rejected Bantustan collaborators and refused to countenance such

117

organizations as Inkatha, founded by Buthelezi in 1975 and based on KwaZulu ethnicity, despite the apparent similarity of emphasis on the distinctiveness of black culture and the need for self-pride (Southall 1981). State harassment of Black Consciousness leaders grew in the 1970s, culminating in the torture and murder of Biko while under police detention in 1977 and the subsequent banning of all Black Consciousness organizations.

Yet despite these limitations, Black Consciousness ideas did find fertile ground in the circumstances of the 1970s. Like other developments in this decade of quietude, it was an important part of the renewed conflicts of subsequent years.

Towards Soweto: protest renewed

The relative calm of the period between 1963 and 1973 was underpinned by some economic improvement in the position of Africans, albeit on a limited scale. Between 1970 and 1972, for the first time, the gap between black and white wages began to narrow, partly because the mines offered slightly higher wages to attract local rather than foreign miners, but mainly because the growth of manufacturing led to a need for skilled employment which was met by black workers.

However, between 1973 and 1976 this process was brought to a halt. A drop in the gold price and heightened inflation mainly caused by an increase in the oil price introduced a period of recession. It was against this background that black protest was renewed by labour conflict. Numerous strikes took place, involving over 200,000 black workers, particularly in Durban and the rest of Natal but also in East London and parts of the Rand. Some national trade union organization took place, but most of the strikes broke out at local factory level in response to specific grievances. This was particularly true in Natal, where the high incidence of strike action was explained by low wages, bad working conditions and ease of communication between workers in different factories who commuted from the nearby KwaZulu homeland and were supported by Buthelezi (Hirson 1979: 142; Friedman 1986: 47–8). Some worker goals were achieved: higher wages and improved working conditions were granted, and the action of these years gave impetus to later recognition of the bargaining powers of black trade unions (see p. 123).

Some writers have argued that this increase in worker militancy explains the township revolts that began in Soweto in June 1976 (Hirson 1979). However, there were other more immediate causes of these upheavals. The early 1970s had seen a major growth in the number of Africans attending schools, although commensurate funding and equipment were lacking, and the difficulty of finding employment after school education increased during the recession of 1973–6. Tensions among school pupils was therefore already high when a new ruling decreed that half of the curriculum in black schools was henceforth to be taught in Afrikaans. In protest 15,000 schoolchildren marched through Soweto. Police confronted the crowd, fired and killed several students. As a result attacks were made on police, administration buildings and beerhalls. Class boycotts, school burnings and counter-attacks and raids by police followed. Within several days the conflict had spread to other townships on the Rand, and in the following weeks also to Cape Town and the eastern Cape. In late August and September school boycotters made successful appeals to workers to stay away from work. Further conflict was caused when police encouraged migrant hostel workers in Soweto to attack pupils who had demanded the closure of the state beerhalls. By the end of the year an official (and doubtless under-estimated) figure was given of 575 dead and 2,389 wounded in the conflicts (Lodge 1983: 330).

The Cillie Commission appointed by the government had a clear explanation. The revolt was the work of outside 'agitators' and bore little relation to real township or youth grievances. Although ANC pamphlets were distributed in Soweto and elsewhere, and the exiled organization later claimed that it had played a major part in organizing the revolt, there is every sign that it was taken by surprise by the events of 1976–7. The detentions and bannings which followed led many township youth to flee from South Africa and join ANC and PAC camps outside the country, but it was only then that active involvement in the nationalist organizations could take place.

The student leaders of Soweto were much more influenced by the Black Consciousness movement, which was particularly influential amongst teachers and student groups in the early 1970s, and this was certainly powerfully expressed in the protests of 'coloured' students in the western Cape in 1976 (Lodge 1983: 333). As Biko said, evidence that Black Consciousness was a force to be reckoned with was 'In one word – Soweto!' (Leatt et al. 1986: 112).

Some further impetus had been given by the success of the anti-colonial movements in neighbouring Mozambique and Angola the

119

previous year, and by the defeat of South African troops who had intervened in Angola in 1975. But the Soweto uprising was not a revolutionary movement. It lacked clear organization and leadership. Despite some contact with workers, the students had no formal links with worker organizations. As some writers have stressed in this regard, the events of 1976 were a missed opportunity (Mafeje 1978).

Yet, as in the case of Sharpeville, the Soweto uprising shocked both South African whites and international opinion. Many foreigners had their first clear image of South Africa formed through vivid television pictures of the Soweto shootings. The anger of a new township generation was palpable and highly threatening to the established order. This and the labour disputes of 1973–6 were reminiscent of the conflicts of the 1940s which apartheid was supposed to have resolved. Although state repression was strong and continued into the next decade, the following years also saw attempts to change the Verwoerdian model. Apartheid was beginning to fail, although this was not fully apparent until the 1980s and it was still to take an unconscionable time to die.

SUGGESTIONS FOR FURTHER READING

Lodge, T. 1983: *Black politics in South Africa since 1945*. London: Longman; Johannesburg: Ravan.
Posel, D. 1991: *The making of apartheid 1948–1961: conflict and compromise*. Oxford: Clarendon.
Stadler, 1987: *The political economy of modern South Africa*. London: Croom Helm; Cape Town: David Philip.

6

Apartheid in Decline

In the course of the late 1970s and the 1980s the rigid Verwoerdian model developed during the heyday of apartheid began to break down. The National Party government experimented with a number of reforms designed to adjust apartheid to changing economic and social circumstances while still retaining a monopoly of political power. But the spiral of resistance and repression intensified. By the mid-1980s virtual civil war existed in many parts of the country, with the army occupying black townships and surrogate vigilante groups adding to the conflict. The state retained control with military power, detentions and increased repression; but the vast majority of South Africa's population was alienated from the state to an unprecedented degree. Meanwhile international condemnation grew and economic sanctions began to bite. The impasse was broken only when the exiled ANC and PAC were unbanned in 1990 and the new State President, F.W. de Klerk, made a qualified commitment to meaningful change. But the decline of apartheid continued to be accompanied by violent conflict and widespread suspicion of state intentions, while economic and social problems became overwhelming in magnitude.

'Total strategy'

In the late 1970s a number of factors led to a change in the policy of the South African state (Moss 1980). First, highly capitalized manufacturing industry now dominated the economy, using complex technology and requiring semi-skilled permanent workers rather than unskilled migrant labourers. In these circumstances, segregation and apartheid, so crucial to the earlier development and growth of industry, were no longer appropriate to the needs of South African capitalism (Lipton 1988).

Economic change also affected the class base of support for the National Party. Afrikaner business interests were now fully integrated into the monopolistic structure of South African industry, while full-scale mechanization of white agriculture produced 'cheque book farmers' linked to business interests rather than struggling producers competing for a limited labour force with urban employers. The cross-class Afrikaner nationalist alliance of the 1940s and 1950s was fracturing: many English-speaking middle-class voters now supported the National Party while Afrikaner workers and small-scale traders and farmers were marginalized. After Vorster's resignation in 1978, following major government financial scandals, the new Prime Minister, P.W. Botha, introduced changes favouring business interests and widened the divisions in the traditional support base of the National Party. The split came with the formation of the right-wing Conservative Party under Andries Treurnicht in 1982, which drew many white working class and blue-collar supporters away from the government. In these circumstances, Botha was obliged to forge a new kind of strategy.

Thirdly, the labour and urban resistance of 1973–7 had caught the government unprepared. It became apparent after Soweto that repression was not enough. Attempts were made to recapture the initiative through reform, particularly by encouraging the development of a black middle class and attempting to win over township residents from African nationalist or radical sympathies.

A final factor explaining the reforms was the unfavourable international response and the threat of sanctions in the aftermath of Soweto, as well as the change of governments in states bordering South Africa, from allied interests to potentially hostile opponents: in Mozambique, Angola and Rhodesia with a similar threat in Namibia as conflict grew between South African forces and guerrilla troops of the South West African People's Organisation (SWAPO). In these circumstances the South African state needed to reassess its public image and its policy strategies.

The outcome was a series of developments between 1979 and 1984 which collectively formulated the policy known as 'total strategy'. Some hint of reform had been given earlier. Prosecution for pass law

122

offences had dropped in number after 1973 at the request of business organizations, including the Afrikaanse Handelsinstituut, although the principle of African labour regulation remained intact (Hindson 1987: 81). Funding for African education had also increased, although insufficiently to prevent student dissatisfaction in 1976. But 'total strategy' went much further. Its rationale was that South Africa was the target of a 'total onslaught' by revolutionaries from inside and outside the country, who could only be combated with a 'total strategy' that 'combin[ed] effective security measures with reformist policies aimed at removing the grievances that revolutionaries could exploit' (Swilling and Phillips 1989: 136). It also aimed to restructure society in ways required by industry, thus combining the economic interests of business, the political interests of the Botha administration and the security interests of the military and security forces: 'an attempt to re-constitute the means of domination in terms favourable to the ruling groups' (Swilling 1988: 5).

Formal links between the National Party and big business were established at the 1979 Carlton Conference in Johannesburg, where Botha pledged his government to support free enterprise and orderly reform. The discourse of free market enterprise was increasingly used by the state in place of overt racial domination, partly as a means of combating the perceived Marxist 'onslaught' but more importantly as a means of establishing ideological hegemony with business support (Greenberg 1987). It marked a major shift from the anti-capitalist rhetoric of the early Afrikaner nationalist movement, and bore little relation to the intense intervention of the state in the political economy of South Africa.

Two government commission reports in 1979 proposed changes to favour stable business development. The Wiehahn report recommended that African rights to trade union membership and registration be recognized. This was done to try to prevent repetition of the wild cat strikes of the 1970s and to formalize, and so control, the labour movement. The Riekert Commission advocated that white job reservation should be dismantled while influx control was still rigorously applied. In this way it maintained the division between permanent city residents and temporary outsiders. Employer demands for greater access to a permanent workforce were thus met, although the principle of controlled African urbanization remained. The pass laws were not abolished until 1986, by which stage a combination of employer needs, the spiralling costs of the immense bureaucratic administration and the belief that repeal would appease international criticism of apartheid persuaded the government to finally remove urban influx controls (Maylam 1990: 80).

The need for semi-skilled black labour was also reflected in the de Lange report on education, published in 1981 (Chisholm 1984). This called for compulsory primary education for all as well as black technical training at secondary and tertiary level. Although the recommendation of a single education authority for all races was rejected by the government, multiracial private schools were permitted. In this, as in other aspects of 'total strategy' policy, the aim was to 'intensify class differentials while reducing racial ones' (Hyslop 1988: 190). This policy was further seen in the removal of many 'petty apartheid' restrictions. Public amenities in large cities, such as hotels, restaurants and theatres, were no longer compulsorily segregated and many opened their doors to all – that is, all who could afford them.

Lack of political representation remained an obstacle to black acceptance of such reform strategies. A second phase of 'total strategy' therefore proposed constitutional changes in an attempt to co-opt sections of the population previously excluded from government. The 1983 'tricameral' constitution created separate parliamentary assemblies for white, coloured and Indian Members of Parliament. Each house controlled its 'own affairs', such as education, health and community administration, but all other matters were still monopolized by the white House of Assembly which retained the overall majority of seats, and the new office of State President, held by Botha, acquired wide-ranging powers.

The tricameral constitution was clearly a means of 'sharing power without losing control' (Murray 1987: 112). Consequently it was boycotted by the vast majority of coloured and Indian voters. Measures which the lesser houses did promote, such as the abolition of the Immorality and Mixed Marriages Acts, were already acceptable to the 'total strategy' policy and indicated the clear move away from the racial control of the 1950s. As with the desegregation of public amenities, they did little to challenge the existing political and social order.

The tricameral constitution made no provision for African participation. The principle remained that constitutional representation for Africans was confined to the homelands. However, recognition of the permanent status of some black township residents had been given in 1977 when Vorster introduced Community Councils to administer township affairs under the aegis of white government officials. In

1982, Botha extended this system by the Black Local Authorities Act which gave Community Councils greater powers of administration. Elected by local residents, councillors were responsible for township administration on budgets raised by local rents and levies. Coinciding with tricameralism, this scheme hoped to create a class of willing collaborators 'in a rather crude effort to defuse black claims to national political power through the substitution of power at grassroots level' (Murray 1987: 123). As with the tricameral elections, township Community Councils had little popular appeal.

Attempts to bolster allegiance to these policies were accompanied by a conscious effort to upgrade townships for those with permanent residence rights. The Urban Foundation, founded with business capital but supported by the state, backed programmes to improve housing and other facilities. In both townships and the rural areas the army was often deployed in community schemes in a campaign to 'win the hearts and minds of the people' (the WHAM policy), although this had a limited effect once the security forces began to suppress opposition (see p. 131).

The role of the army was a further important component of 'total strategy'. Botha, previously the Minister of Defence, gave an important role to the armed forces within policy making as part of security against the 'total onslaught'. The State Security Council, established in 1972 as an advisory body to the Cabinet, now gained greater powers under the new Minister of Defence, General Magnus Malan, including that of control over intelligence and security work. By 1980 it was observed that 'in many ways [the SSC] is already an alternative Cabinet' (Murray 1987: 40).

In addition to the WHAM campaign to stem the 'total onslaught' within the country, Botha attempted to defuse opposition from potentially hostile countries in the wider southern African region. His hope of creating a 'constellation of states' linked to South Africa by trade was foiled by the organization of the frontline states against South African influence, but the security forces then mounted a campaign of destabilization. Direct military incursions accompanied indirect support of dissident armed movements such as RENAMO in Mozambique and UNITA in Angola, while raids were made on centres which the South African state claimed housed ANC guerillas in Lesotho, Swaziland, Zimbabwe and Botswana. In Namibia, South African occupation continued and a bitter guerrilla war was fought with the nationalist SWAPO (Davies and O'Meara 1984). In 1984 the results of this policy met some success with the signing of the

Nkomati non-aggression accord with Mozambique, by which the Maputo government agreed to expel ANC guerrilla camps from its territory in return for the ending of South African support for RENAMO.

'Total strategy' was thus as much a reformulation of apartheid as a reform. Its purpose was to maintain white political hegemony while restructuring some aspects of the social and political order to counter the threat of revolutionary opposition. This was abundantly clear to many of the state's opponents, who resisted 'total strategy' with renewed energy.

Resistance and repression

'Total strategy' was intended to defuse protest outbreaks of the kind that had occurred in the 1970s, and to bring economic and political stability to South Africa. It had precisely the opposite effect.

The economy failed to recover the growth rates it had shown in the 1960s and early 1970s. Despite a brief recuperation between 1978 and 1980, subsequent years saw a fall in the gold price, a balance of payments crisis and dependence on loans from the International Monetary Fund and foreign bankers. Inflation and unemployment soared in 1982, and again in 1984. The standard of living of all South Africans fell: black poverty became even more acute than ever.

These circumstances did not favour a state campaign to 'win hearts and minds'. The recession was accompanied by heightened opposition to 'total strategy' policies. Many of the Botha reforms produced consequences unintended by the state (Friedman 1986). For instance, the relaxation of pass controls led to an unprecedented move of Africans into the cities. This was particularly evident in Cape Town, where the ending of legislated preference for coloured workers gave greater possibilities for African employment. Large squatter camps grew up on the outskirts of the city, particularly at Crossroads. At first, they were ruthlessly destroyed as the dwellings of 'illegal' incomers by the ironically named Department of Co-operation and Development. But by 1984 the government conceded the rights of squatters to stay in the region and plans were laid for the building of a large new township at Khayelitsha. The attempt to distinguish between permanent residents and temporary outsiders was collapsing here as in many other cities.

Another unintended development was the emergence of powerful trade unions. The proper recognition of African union negotiating mechanisms led to a massive growth in membership, particularly among migrant workers hitherto excluded from union representation. Falling real wages and poor working conditions produced a number of strikes in the early 1980s. But action went further than local factory issues. In 1982, spurred by the death in detention of Neil Aggett, the Transvaal organizer of the Food and Canning Workers Union, many unions came together to organize campaigns which represented broader political interests and protested against state policies. Thus in November 1984 a major stayaway was organized on the Rand backed by union and community groups. Large-scale union affiliations were being formed with political allegiances. The largest was the Congress of South African Trade Unions (COSATU), launched in 1985 and following a broadly Charterist position. The Azanian Confederation of Trade Unions (AZACTU) took a position more in tune with Black Consciousness lines, and in 1986 the United Workers Union of South Africa (UWUSA) was established under the aegis of the more conservative Inkatha movement. The point was that unions were now at the forefront of the political struggle. Although there were debates within the unions over the advisability of involvement in wider populist politics, and fears that worker issues might thus be submerged, coordinated action between the federated unions and student and community organizations took place with increasing frequency from the mid-1980s. Far from taming the labour movement, the Wiehahn reforms had politicized it (Webster 1988).

The context for this was heightened popular resistance and mobilization on a scale which exceeded even that of the 1950s and 1976–7 and which took new forms and goals. In 1980 coloured school students in the western Cape boycotted classes to protest against the use of army servicemen as teachers and to demand free education for everyone and not for whites alone. Links were made with striking meat workers in Cape Town. Boycott action spread to the Rand and the eastern Cape, where it meshed with demands for the ending of homeland citizenship. Although the boycotts were broken by police action by the end of the year, these episodes provided a link between the uprising of 1976–7 and the more widespread resistance of the mid-1980s.

The catalyst to this was the tricameral constitution and the Black Local Government Act. Both measures made it absolutely clear that the Botha government was attempting to restructure apartheid rather than to dismantle it, and that the African majority would continue to be permanently excluded from central government. White control would be entrenched but the state hoped that the new system would be more acceptable both locally and internationally. New oppositional organizations emerged to demonstrate the fallacy of this belief.

Early in 1983, the National Forum (NF) was established, bringing together supporters of Black Consciousness in the Azanian People's Organisation (AZAPO) and the non-collaborationist tradition of the western Cape Unity Movement. Its 'Manifesto of the Azanian People' opposed all alliances with ruling class parties, demanded the immediate establishment of 'a democratic, anti-racist worker republic in Azania' and defined the struggle for national liberation as 'directed against the system of racial capitalism which holds the people of Azania in bondage for the benefit of the small minority of white capitalists and their allies, the white workers and the reactionary sections of the black middle class' (Davies et al. 1988: 454).

Such a policy was a rejection of the broader populist Charterist tradition which was represented in the foundation of the United Democratic Front (UDF) in the same year. The UDF called for rejection of the apartheid state, boycott of the tricameral system and acceptance of the Freedom Charter principles (see pp. 105–6). The campaign had dramatic results: only a small percentage of 'coloured' and Indian voters cast their poll, and many others refused even to register. The tricameral system was thus denied legitimacy from the start.

Both the NF and the UDF were loosely knit confederations of church, community and trade union organizations, rather than political parties. Their differences lay in their ideologies, with the NF regarding worker interests as paramount and criticizing the UDF for its 'petty bourgeois' leadership and its populist multi-class character. The Black Consciousness strand in NF thinking was apparent in the reluctance of some of its supporters to admit white dominated organizations such as the National Union of South African Students (NUSAS). However, those from the Unity tradition rejected any policy which recognized race. Indeed the involvement of AZAPO members in the NF showed how the Black Consciousness movement had moved decisively towards workerist positions since the days of Biko.

The UDF acquired by far the largest number of affiliates and the highest public profile, and was only really challenged by the NF in the western Cape. The UDF drew on a wide range of local community

128

organizations across the country, and particularly in the Transvaal and the eastern Cape. Swilling (1988) has argued that its Charterist position did not preclude working-class membership and indeed leadership. Certainly, as protest developed in the course of 1984–6, the organizations affiliated to the UDF gave it an increasingly radical character.

The UDF also worked more actively to recruit support to its affiliated organizations at a local level. Its campaign to obtain a million signatures for a petition against apartheid in the aftermath of the tricameral elections in 1984 failed to attain its numerical goal, partly because of police harassment and confiscation of signed papers, but 'it did, for the first time, provide township activists with a vehicle for some solid door-to-door organizing' (Swilling 1988: 101).

By 1985 this was bearing fruit in a series of local campaigns, including bus and rent boycotts, school protests and worker stay-aways. Although local circumstances varied, a common focus of township resistance was the Community Councils and those coun-cillors who accepted office and were branded as collaborators in the apartheid system. Economic pressures also undermined the position of the councils. Not only were they politically unacceptable, but their dependence on local funding and their role as collectors of rents and unpopular service charges made them vulnerable to protests against increases at a time of recession. Tensions were heightened by accusations of corruption and malpractice. Such issues mobilized township residents of all ages and meshed with student protests and boycotts.

It was primarily resistance to increases in rent and service charges that led to a major rebellion in the townships of the Vaal triangle between September and November 1984 (Seekings 1988). Protest spread to other parts of the Transvaal, with attacks on councillors and their homes as well as government buildings, homes of police and beerhalls. A number of councillors resigned under such threats to their lives, but the uprising continued with student and worker protests at the fore. By 1985 township conflict had spread to the Orange Free State, the eastern Cape and finally to Cape Town and Natal.

State repression only fuelled further opposition. On Sharpeville Day, 1985, police opened fire on a funeral procession in Uitenhage in the eastern Cape, killing twenty people in an episode which bore strong resemblance to the events twenty-five years earlier. This provoked renewed school boycotts throughout the country and clashes between township youth and police. By July the situation had reached such proportions that the government declared a State of Emergency in many regions, extending the power of arbitrary detention without trial and indemnifying the security forces against any charge of malpractice. With a brief break in 1986, emergency regulations were extended throughout the country and remained in place until 1990.

The conflicts of 1984–6 marked a new phase in South African popular resistance. In many townships throughout the country civil government collapsed, to be replaced by alternative, unofficial organizations calling for 'people's power'. In many cases, as in 1976–7, the initiative was taken by youth organizations, although they drew support from a wider sector of the community than was the case previously. More effective links were made between students and workers, particularly in the Vaal triangle and in the eastern Cape. Street committees organized coordinated actions such as rent boycotts and consumer boycotts of white businesses to persuade their owners to support calls for desegregation and lessening of state oppression. Moreover, this happened in hitherto unpoliticized small towns in platteland South Africa as much as in the large metropolitan townships.

The oppositional organizations played an important part in creating an alternative national political culture which transcended local issues and gave a sense of common purpose. In this the UDF's Charterist line was crucial. In many townships the ideals of the Freedom Charter provided the focus for action and political organization. A case study of Youth Congress activists in the Alexandra township near Johannesburg shows that in practice this might not always have penetrated very deeply, although debates over populist and workerist issues and clashes with AZAPO supporters were part of the linking of local issues of rent and school boycotts with a wider national framework (Carter 1991).

A further important development was the massive increase in support for the exiled ANC, not only in its earlier regions of strength such as the eastern Cape and the Transvaal but also in the western Cape where historically its position had been weaker (Bundy 1987b). Songs of praise to Mandela and Tambo, study of ANC underground literature, ANC flags draped across coffins at the many funerals of activists killed by the security forces and shouts of 'Viva' (the Lusophone rally cry used at ANC camps in Angola and Mozambique) gave visible signs of ANC resurgence within the townships. In this the

UDF played a crucial role, replacing the predominantly Black Consciousness ideology of the mid-1970s. Guerrilla infiltration by Umkhonto we Sizwe members also increased, with attacks on power stations and even the military headquarters of the Defence Force in Pretoria. By 1985–6 a number of delegations of South African business, student, church and trade union leaders were visiting the ANC headquarters in Lusaka (Lodge 1988). The ANC was widely recognized as the South African government-in-exile.

By late 1985, the spiral of popular resistance and state repression had reached new heights. Violence in townships was directed not only against councillors but also suspected informers. In some areas youth operated 'people's courts' to punish breakers of the consumer boycott, and in some widely publicized cases death sentences were carried out on state collaborators by necklacing, that is placing burning tyres around their necks. There was a widespread but mistaken belief that the state was about to collapse. Hence the slogan among boycotting students of 'liberation before education' (Bundy 1987b). Only at the end of 1985 did the National Education Crisis Committee, formed by parent, teacher and youth bodies, change this call to one of demand for alternative 'People's Education' (Hyslop 1988).

Despite such challenges to the state it was clear by 1986 that revolution was not just around the corner. Local authorities could be overthrown but central government was more powerful. The state hit back hard. The army was deployed in the townships alongside the police from October 1984, thousands of activists were detained and organizations such as the UDF and AZAPO were banned. Running street battles took place throughout 1985–6 in many townships but stones and burning barricades were ultimately no match for heavily armed security forces. With the aid of Emergency powers, the army and police had crushed the rebellion by 1987.

In the process a high degree of militarization had taken place. Massive amounts of the state budget went on defence, most of it deployed internally. Conscripted whites fought a civil war in the townships, white schools were infused with security force propaganda and military training and the State Security Council played an ever-increasing role in the formation of government policy (Evans and Phillips 1988). After 1986 the National Security Management System, headed by the Minister of Defence, General Magnus Malan, set up a web of local administrative bodies under military and police command to act as 'security controls' (Morris and Padayachee 1988).

This did not go unopposed amongst white South Africans. The use of the military in civil action led to heightened objection by some conscripted national servicemen. The End Conscription Campaign (ECC), founded in 1983, gained wider support after the deployment of troops in townships, and although its impact was largely limited to a few liberal English-speakers, it was sufficiently threatening to the state to be subject to harassment and final banning in 1988 (Nathan 1989).

The state not only intervened directly, it also encouraged reactionary vigilante action against township activists. Vigilantes emerged in 1985 to protect township councillors, police and traders but widened their activities to include attacks on a number of anti-apartheid organization members, in both townships and the Bantustans. This was portrayed in the media as 'black on black' violence, but it is clear that vigilante groups received support from the police for whom they were a convenient means of countering protest. The attacks came from within communities, removing the stigma of aggression from the security forces but giving them a rationale for staying in the townships (Haysom 1989).

A particularly dramatic example of vigilante action was that of the 'Witdoeke' (named after the white headbands with which they identified themselves), who appeared in Cape Town squatter camps. In May and June of 1986 they destroyed shacks at Crossroads and other camps, while police stood by and allegedly intervened to protect them from retaliatory action by residents. Although originating under the patronage of local councillors and self-appointed landlords, many vigilantes by the end of 1986 were formally incorporated into the security forces as 'community guards' and 'kitskonstabel' police auxiliaries ('instant constables').

Community conflicts sometimes reflected deeper tensions. In August 1985 violence erupted in Inanda, near Durban, which was depicted by the media as based on ethnic conflict between Indian shop and property owners and African tenants and squatters, thus evoking memories of the 1949 Durban riots (see p. 104). Certainly ethnic division was highlighted by Inanda's circumstances. An area of freehold property ownership since the nineteenth century, many Indians had established farms and businesses in Inanda and some were landlords with predominantly African tenants. Increased population led to severe overcrowding and poverty by the 1980s. Tensions rose when Inanda was scheduled for incorporation into KwaZulu, with claims that rents were being increased (Hughes 1987). But the conflict was also based on political competition. Vigilantes took action against UDF-affiliated youth in Inanda, not in support of Indian property-owners but as supporters of Inkatha.

Clashes between UDF groups and Inkatha grew in intensity from the mid-1980s. Inkatha was originally established in the 1920s as a Zulu ethnic movement to stem the greater radicalism of the ICU (see p. 82). Revived by Buthelezi, the Chief Minister of the KwaZulu homeland in 1975, it had grown by 1980 to be the largest African political organization in the country – although with so many others banned that was hardly a major achievement, and its membership was confined primarily to rural areas of KwaZulu.

Buthelezi trod an uneasy line. He refused independence for KwaZulu, thus seriously setting back the Bantustan strategy, and initially presented himself as the internal wing of the ANC, demanding the release of ANC leaders before considering negotiation with the government. However, Buthelezi and Inkatha, rejected by Black Consciousness supporters as collaborators, had by the early 1980s also increasingly moved away from ANC positions by rejecting protest politics and international sanctions. For this Buthelezi won much support from liberal whites. The opposition Progressive Federal Party, for example, approved of his plans for a federal state structure in which KwaZulu would play a major role. He also increasingly found favour with the government. However, he lost the initiative in the 1984–6 revolt, and forfeited the conciliatory role which he hoped to obtain amongst Africans (Southall 1981).

Inkatha emphasized 'the maintenance of patriarchal and hierarchical values' which it presented as traditional aspects of African political culture (McCaul 1988: 158–9). But it expanded its support outside traditional rural areas in the course of the early 1980s. KwaZulu administrators and teachers were almost universally members, and the Inkatha Youth Brigade worked actively in KwaZulu schools. The appeal of Zulu ethnicity was used to attract workers both in Durban and on the Rand to unions federated to UWUSA, established in 1986 as a rival to the UDF-oriented COSATU.

By this time Inkatha's split with the ANC-Charterist tradition was complete, and mutual recriminations between UDF and Inkatha took place. Certainly the presence of Inkatha explained the low support that the UDF obtained in many parts of rural Natal, although in squatter settlements and townships around Durban and Pietermaritzburg support for the rival organizations was more divided. By mid-1985 political tensions ran high, meshing with community conflicts in

Inanda as well as in the Durban townships of KwaMashu and Umlazi. This was fuelled by the assassination of Victoria Mxenge, a prominent lawyer sympathetic to the UDF, and the subsequent call for a boycott and stayaway by COSATU and UDF-affiliated youth organizations. Inkatha opposed such actions which it regarded as a UDF-inspired recruiting drive in the contested territory of Natal townships, and Inkatha vigilante groups moved in.

The conflict in Natal grew in intensity when elsewhere it was suppressed. In 1987–8 civil war existed in the area around Pieter-maritzburg. Long-standing rivalry between Inkatha and ANC/UDF supporters was certainly the cause of this, with attacks and counter-attacks in which the violence of Inkatha was often ignored or even encouraged by the police while UDF activists were detained (Kentridge 1990). But the war also took place in one of the most impoverished regions of the country and competition for scarce resources added to the problem. Complex local power and clientage relationships played a role; as Gwala (1989) has shown, some private African freeholders in areas around Pietermaritzburg resisted Inkatha to assert their independence from KwaZulu government control over their lands. Generational conflicts and the weakening of the more traditional patriarchal ties in some parts of Natal played a part in the Inkatha/UDF divide (Campbell 1992). The UDF–ANC 'comrades' were most often associated with new kinds of community mobilization in the townships and villages (Sitas 1992).

One thing about the Natal war was clear. It was not the ethnic clash of 'Zulu' versus 'Xhosa' as claimed by the state and the international media in its depiction of 'black on black violence'. And increasingly allegations of state support for Inkatha gave rise to suspicion that the government was actively encouraging vigilante action.

1987–1993: stalemate and breakthrough

The resistance of the mid-1980s destroyed utterly the 'total strategy' tactics of the Botha government. Tricameralism and African urban councils had been firmly rejected by the demand for 'People's Power'. The campaign to win hearts and minds was in tatters, with thousands in detention without prospect of trial and an occupying army in the townships.

134

It was not only the disenfranchised who rejected the government and its policies. By 1985 those business interests which had cautiously allied themselves with the reformist state in 1979 were now bitterly critical of it. A turning point came in August of that year, when expectations raised by Pik Botha, the Foreign Minister, of an imminent announcement of meaningful reform to meet internal demands and stave off foreign sanctions were quashed by an angry and unrepentant P.W. Botha. His 'Rubicon address', delivered in the full glare of massive international publicity, firmly rejected any notion of majority rule or response to foreign pressure.

The response was immediate. Loans granted by foreign banks in 1982 were now called in, with no facility for renewal. As a result the rand collapsed, and the Johannesburg Stock Exchange was temporarily closed. These events 'spurred South African business leaders on to the offensive' (Mann 1988: 80). Within a month leading business directors were visiting the ANC in Lusaka. International condemnation of South Africa grew even stronger in intensity, with the United States and most Commonwealth and European Community nations speeding up disinvestment and economic sanctions. Only Thatcher's refusal to follow this trend gave continued openings for South African trade and communication links.

Other key props of the South African political economy were also collapsing by 1987. Although the resistance of the mid-1980s centred on townships, rural opposition also played an important part in defeating government policies. For instance in 1986 the UDF set up an effective local branch in Lebowa, where traditions of opposition to chiefs appointed by the government went back to the Sekhukhuneland revolt of the 1950s (see p. 102). With high levels of malnutrition, drought and unemployment, UDF activists were able to mobilize a wide sector of the rural population against the Bantustan officials (Lodge and Nasson 1991: 117–26). In KwaNdebele similar mass opposition led to a rejection of independence in 1986 (Transvaal Rural Action Committee 1988). Together with the long-standing refusal of KwaZulu to take independence, this effectively brought a halt to the Bantustan strategy.

With the collapse of 'total strategy', the government seemed bankrupted of ideas, relying on internal repression and international bravado. In May 1986 a high-ranking Commonwealth delegation (a concession granted to Thatcher by Commonwealth leaders) arrived in South Africa to investigate the situation and talk to the government. But while the delegation was still in the country, its visit was

135

undermined by South African raids on supposed ANC bases in Harare, Lusaka and Gaborone. International condemnation rose to still greater heights, and even Thatcher was appalled.

By 1987 a stalemate existed. Writing in the following year one academic described the situation as one 'in which the inability of dissidents to overthrow the hegemony of the state is countered by the incapability of the state to eliminate dissidence completely' (Frankel 1988: 280). The state had lost the initiative but no-one else had the power to seize it. The tricameral election of 1987 returned the Nationalists to the white House of Assembly but with a right-wing Conservative Party opposition. The disaffection of white workers and farmers, squeezed by the slumping economy and falling real wage levels was becoming a serious factor in this right-wing resurgence. Reform was certainly no longer on Botha's cards. With the banning of many organizations, virtually the only legal voice of opposition came from the churches, especially from the new Anglican Archbishop of Cape Town, Desmond Tutu.

The breaking of this stalemate came from an unexpected source. In August 1989, Botha was forced to step down on the demand of members of his Cabinet, following his public rebuke of the Transvaal leader of the National Party, F.W. de Klerk, for planning a visit to the ANC in Lusaka. De Klerk replaced him and led the government into a tricameral election where it lost seats to both the Conservatives on the right and the Democratic Party to its left.

Resistance to government had taken a new direction in the course of 1989. In contrast to the confrontation of youth and other activists in the streets of the townships, the leaders of the UDF and COSATU allied in what was known as the Mass Democratic Movement (MDM) called for a campaign of mass civil disobedience to challenge segregated facilities such as hospitals, schools and beaches. Unlike the rather disparate defiance campaigns of the 1950s, the actions of 1989 were well coordinated. They were also successful in bringing about desegregation. Lodge and Nasson (1991: 110–11) suggest that this may have been because desegregation was already being planned by the government and such challenges were little threat to its authority. After de Klerk's takeover, police attacks on defiance campaigners were markedly toned down. In September and October a number of peaceful marches took place in the centre of the major cities, joined by many whites, in protest against the State of Emergency and the powers of the security forces. No action was taken against the demonstrators. They did not seem to greatly threaten the state, although by the end of the year the initiative clearly lay with the MDM.

But in his opening address to Parliament on 2 February 1990, de Klerk made a dramatic move. He announced the unbanning of the ANC, PAC and South African Communist Party, and in the following weeks released many political prisoners, including Nelson Mandela. In 1991 key pieces of apartheid legislation were repealed, such as the Group Areas Act, the Land Act and the Population Registration Act. And later that year, the government entered into formal negotiations with a range of parties, including the ANC, at the Convention for a Democratic South Africa (CODESA), committing itself to a new constitution to give democratic rights in a single unitary state.

What had brought about this complete volte-face by the National Party government? Popular protest and international condemnation were certainly part of the broad background. But the overriding factor was the profound economic crisis of the country. Foreign sanctions were beginning to bite severely. As the Governor of the South African Reserve Bank warned in May 1989,

> if adequate progress is not made in the field of political and constitutional reform, South Africa's relationships with the rest of the world are unlikely to improve . . . In that event South Africa will probably remain a capital-exporting and debt-repaying country for years . . . In such circumstances, the average standard of living in South Africa will at best rise only slowly.
>
> (Terreblanche and Nattrass 1990: 18)

Botha's 'reforms' had been unable to overcome the effects of economic isolation. Moreover, the structural inequalities of apartheid were too glaring to be ignored and were detrimental to the whole economy. As elsewhere in the late 1980s, technological changes were making unskilled labour redundant. Most blacks, and increasing numbers of whites, were unemployed and unemployable. New capital investment was lacking. Prices were rising and real wages, for those who were earning them, were falling sharply. The relative national prosperity which accompanied apartheid in the 1960s had vanished for ever. It had taken almost two decades for the state to recognize that political reform was a necessary precondition to any attempt at economic recovery. Without this, the continuing spiral of ever worsening poverty, disaffection and repression was inevitable.

In these circumstances, the new State President and his Cabinet made a political gamble in order to break through the stalemate and regain the initiative. Threats from the growing Conservative Party in an all-white electorate needed to be pre-empted. De Klerk was apparently told by his security advisors in the course of 1989 that the ANC had been sufficiently weakened by attacks on its frontline bases and on its internal underground structures to be a controllable force if unbanned (Giliomee 1992: 33–4). It appeared that an alliance between a 'new-look' National Party, drawing in white voters from the left and centre of Parliament, and the conservative Inkatha Freedom Party with its predominently Zulu membership could win over a significant percentage of the population and give the Nationalists a share, if not a monopoly, of power in a democratic, and hence internationally supported, government.

This belief was bolstered by trends outside South Africa. The collapse of Communist states throughout eastern Europe and in the Soviet Union following the Gorbachev 'revolution' and the general discrediting of socialism that seemed to accompany it, indicated that the ANC and its SACP allies might be weakened in South Africa as well and that 'free market' ideology could triumph. Moreover, the end of the Cold War removed the threat of the 'Communist onslaught' that for so long had played a major part in 'total strategy' thinking. The demotion of the military in de Klerk's cabinet marked a move away from such policies.

In 1989 democratic elections had been held in Namibia, from which South Africa had finally agreed to withdraw after its military vulnerability was exposed in Angola by Cuban, Angolan and SWAPO forces in the preceding year. Although SWAPO won a majority, its support was by no means unanimous and the more conservative opposition won a much higher proportion of seats than had been the case in the Zimbabwean independence elections of 1979. Radical African nationalism seemed on the wane. De Klerk evidently hoped that he could regain legitimacy and play an important role in a majority government which would be more conservative than had seemed likely at any earlier stage. And in shifting away from single-party rule to multi-party democracy, South Africa was part of a broader trend taking place in other parts of the continent (Etherington 1992).

Certainly de Klerk's actions did not represent a surrender on the part of National Party government. Rather it was a bid to regain the initiative. Soon after Mandela's release the ANC agreed to participate in negotiations with the state and to suspend the armed struggle. As a result, by March 1992 tangible benefits had been obtained for the government. Some economic sanctions were lifted, sports boycotts were removed with South Africa's participation in the Barcelona Olympic Games, and international political acceptance was achieved for the first time since the mid-1970s. The effect of this was demonstrated by a white referendum in which 69 per cent of voters supported negotiations at CODESA. Right-wing claims that de Klerk lacked white support were seen to be unfounded.

But there was little agreement about the form that a future political settlement should take. After the referendum victory de Klerk became more assertive, particularly when opinion polls suggested he was gaining coloured, Indian and even some African support whereas the ANC was having difficulty transforming itself from a liberation movement into a political party. The National Party insisted on the protection of minority rights and the election of an interim government of national unity in which it would secure some power for at least a decade.

The ANC faced other difficulties. In 1990 Buthelezi had converted Inkatha to a political party, the Inkatha Freedom Party, at which stage many anticipated a NP–IFP alliance or possibly an electoral coalition. More significantly, violence between Inkatha supporters and the now legalized ANC and its allies increased in intensity in Natal, especially on the Rand, and in other areas of the country. As in Natal during the late 1980s, this conflict was more nuanced than the ethnic battle depicted in the media. The increasing flow of migrants to the cities after the lifting of influx control created new social tensions and economic struggles in townships and in informal 'squatter' settlements which meshed with political rivalries (Sapire 1992). A particular cause of conflict on the Rand was the tension between migrant hostel dwellers, many from Inkatha-dominated rural Natal, and local township residents. This tension was heightened by unemployment and fuelled by ethnic mobilization (Segal 1992). Accusations made by the ANC that a 'third force' was at work became credible when it was revealed that the government had provided Inkatha with financial backing and military training.

Revelations of this kind increased suspicion and mistrust between the government and the ANC. By 1992 the ANC leadership was under growing criticism from its grassroots membership for talking to the enemy while killings continued in the townships. In June, ANC members attending a funeral in the Transvaal township of Boipatong,

139

were attacked by Inkatha members supported by the police. The ANC withdrew from negotiations in protest and demanded a full investigation into the causes of violence and a firm check on the activities of the police and security forces. In an attempt to deflect international and local criticism, De Klerk appointed a commission led by Justice Goldstone to investigate the causes of violence. Its investigations and press revelations deeply implicated the state security forces.

Tensions increased in subsequent months as the ANC threatened mass action campaigns. A march of ANC supporters to the Ciskei homeland capital of Bisho led to shootings by Ciskei forces and revealed the complexity of conflict in rural as well as urban areas. But the problems facing the country were not only political. Caught up in the general world depression of the early 1990s and lacking the necessary boost of capital investment for which de Klerk had hoped, the economy continued to slump. Under these conditions the optimism created in 1990 quickly evaporated. Yet it was clear that the clock could not be turned back to the apartheid era. Neither the government nor the oppositional movements could gain from a long-term stalemate.

In these circumstances ANC and government leaders maintained a degree of contact and in September 1992 they agreed in a Record of Understanding to resume negotiations. In 1993 a new forum was established at Kempton Park. Both parties had recognized their strengths and limitations in the aftermath of CODESA's breakdown, and the National Party was quietly abandoning its insistence on minority electoral protection.

But such bilateral agreements alienated Buthelezi, who was further offended by the government's abandonment of a close alliance after its covert military and financial support of Inkatha had been exposed. Buthelezi refused to attend Kempton Park and the IFP held out against a unitary constitutional system, demanding instead federal and ethnic particularism in KwaZulu–Natal under a revamped Zulu monarchy. In this Inkatha found allies in the rulers of Bophutatswana and Ciskei as well as in the right-wing Conservative Party. Together they formed the Concerned South Africans Group (COSAG) and opposed ANC and NP agreements in the negotiations.

Opposition also came from the PAC and AZAPO who accused the ANC of being a bourgeois organization that was selling out the interests of the black working class. The PAC was implicated in

140

attacks on whites in both rural and urban areas, made by the guerilla Azanian People's Liberation Army (APLA).

Soon after the convening of the Kempton Park negotiations this fragile balance was seriously disrupted by the assassination of the popular SACP and Umkhonto we Sizwe leader, Chris Hani, by a right-wing gunman. Angered by this, and frustrated by the lack of any meaningful change since 1990, youth protested throughout the country, bringing the spectre of violent opposition into the centre of several cities. Many of them ignored Mandela's appeal for calm and appeared to be either abandoning the ANC for the PAC, or demanding a more radical policy from ANC leaders. The spectre of extreme right-wing violence and the frustrations of an alienated black youth had reached a critical level. Time was rapidly running out, both for the government to achieve a settlement in which it could retain some control, and for the ANC to retain its grassroot support.

This new sense of urgency acted as a catalyst at Kempton Park. An election date was finally set for April 1994 and the National Party, alarmed at polls which showed a significant decrease in its support, conceded the appointment of a Transitional Executive Council to supervise the intervening period alongside the government and also the election of a transitional government for five years without any minority or federal safeguards. As a result Inkatha walked out of the negotiations and the Conservative Party and other right-wing movements also boycotted Kempton Park. Some right-wing extremists led by the Afrikaner Weerstand Beweging (Afrikaner Resistance Movement), which had been formed in 1973 under the fanatic Eugene Terreblanche, now threatened civil war if majority rule was implemented, although their actual power remained to be tested.

The other main players at Kempton Park nonetheless proceeded to draw up an interim constitution. For five years South Africa was to be ruled by a democratically elected Government of National Unity, consisting of all parties who won enough votes under a proportional representation system for a place in the 400 seat National Assembly. Those parties obtaining over 5 per cent of the national vote were entitled to representation in the Cabinet which was led by an executive President elected by the majority of members. Any party obtaining more than 80 seats was entitled to a Deputy President. Such a system seemed likely to secure a Deputy Presidency for de Klerk under Mandela's Presidency, thus reconciling the interests of both key players. The right of veto in the Cabinet or National Assembly by minority parties was denied but a permanent constitution

141

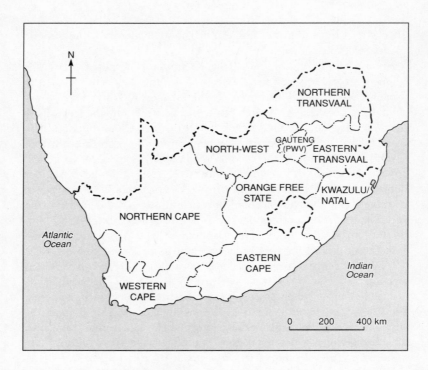

Map 5   South African Provinces, 1994

was to be drawn up by the new government supported by at least 66 per cent of its members. A Bill of Rights guaranteed fundamental freedoms such as racial and gender equality. Nine new provinces replaced the former system of provinces and homelands, each with its own legislature, although their powers were vague and their funding dependent on central government. This fell far short of a federal system.

Some modification to this constitution was made in early 1994 in an attempt to draw in both the white right wing and Inkatha. Promise of a double ballot (one for central and one for provincial government) and the formation of an Afrikaner *volksraad* (although with no powers) led to a right-wing split and to a leading army general, Constand Viljoen, registering a political party, the Freedom Front (FF), to contest the election, while the Conservative Party continued its boycott of the election.

It was less easy to woo Buthelezi back into the fold. Violence in Natal continued unabated and Inkatha refused to permit voter education or electioneering in KwaZulu. A state of emergency was declared in Natal and the spectre of continued civil war loomed large in the weeks before the election. Desperate mediation, both government and international, failed to persuade Buthelezi to participate until just one week before polling day. Only then did he realize that the election was going to take place without him. Moreover, it appears that attempts by the state and the ANC to weaken the link between him and the Zulu king, Goodwill Zwelithini, threatened his ability to stand out as the representative of a united Zulu separatism.

Inkatha's final participation was also encouraged by the collapse of the other homeland members of COSAG. South African citizenship had been restored to all homeland residents in order to enable them to vote in the election and most homeland leaders had backed this. Lucas Mangope of Bophutatswana and Oupa Gqozo of the Ciskei still held out against reunification and the loss of their privileged positions. But the reality of the forthcoming loss of financial support from a democratic government in Pretoria led to civil servant and army strikes in both areas. In Bophutatswana, Mangope was overthrown only a month before the election. A threatened AWB 'invasion' to support him failed ignominiously, breaking the mystique of a right-wing military threat. Thus by polling day most of the key players had been incorporated into the election process.

The election campaign focussed primarily on the personalities of the party leaders, particularly Mandela and de Klerk, both of whom were more popular than their respective parties. Both the ANC and the NP consciously sought to present a new image to the electorate. The ANC played down its role as a liberation movement and emphasized its careful plans for reconstruction and development in order to counteract accusations that its leaders were inexperienced in government. Although still broadly following the principles of the Freedom Charter, it also played down socialism and entertained free market ideas. The NP stressed de Klerk's role as South Africa's saviour and the extent to which it had turned its back on apartheid. Other parties made little impact in the campaign. The PAC was underfunded, disorganized and overshadowed by the ANC, whereas the DP found its role as a liberal opposition party increasingly irrelevant and its ideals taken over by the more prominent NP.

143

On polling days the violence predicted by the world media failed to materialize and was replaced by images of patient queues and euphoric voters as almost 20 million South Africans participated. Indeed, the election was a cathartic breaking point with South Africa's past and worthy of Mandela's description of it as a 'small miracle' by late twentieth-century standards. But the logistical difficulties of the election were formidable, particularly those caused by the last-minute participation of Inkatha. Results were delayed and accusations of electoral malpractice abounded, especially in KwaZulu-Natal. The final results reflected a compromise between contesting parties over disputed cases.

But the results were recognized by all parties, not least because they reflected an ideal situation for a consensus government. The ANC won 62.6 per cent of the national vote, large enough to give it a convincing majority but just short of the 66 per cent required for it to unilaterally write a new constitution. The NP scored 20.4 per cent ensuring de Klerk his position as one of the Deputy Presidents alongside the ANC's Thabo Mbeki, and the IFP obtained 10.5 per cent giving Buthelezi a seat in the Cabinet as Minister of Home Affairs. Other parties fared less well. The Freedom Front obtained 2.2 per cent, enough for it to win nine seats in the National Assembly but failing to overcome the split within the white right wing, whereas the DP and PAC each obtained less than 2 per cent of the national vote. The only other party to obtain enough votes for seats in Parliament was a hastily formed fundamentalist Christian party.

At regional level the ANC swept the board in six of the nine provinces and narrowly obtained control in the Northern Cape. But it lost KwaZulu-Natal to Inkatha and the Western Cape to the NP. The Natal result was highly contentious, but grudgingly accepted to prevent threats of continued violence. The Western Cape was the only province where Africans formed a minority: most voters supported the NP including many coloureds who were alarmed by the spectre raised by the NP in the election campaign of ANC affirmative action for Africans in jobs and housing. Indeed, it appears that most South Africans did vote on racial grounds with the large majority of whites backing the NP, DP or FF and Africans supporting the ANC, IFP or PAC. While the balance of power between the parties at national level achieved the purpose of wide representation in government this division of voter allegiance also reflected the deep divisions of South African society.

Mandela's inauguration as State President marked a new era of democratic government for South Africa, although one of an uneasy combination of wide political differences. Its new flag, which combined the old colours with those of African nationalism, and the use of both the old national anthem and the liberation hymn Nkosi Sikelela iAfrika (God Bless Africa) was symbolic of this combination. But granting everybody the vote did not, of course, remove apartheid. The legacy of profound economic and social deprivation remained. The ANC's Reconstruction and Development plan was adopted but little change took place in the lives of the majority of South Africans. The new government was accused by many of its supporters of being more concerned with retaining the support of local and international business interests than with making meaningful social reforms. Political stability in a potentially volatile situation was prized over social transformation. Although the government may have changed, existing civil servants, the army and the police were guaranteed their jobs. Attempts to amalgamate the South African Defence Force with Umkhonto we Sizwe and APLA guerilla forces met with considerable difficulties. Legislation passed in 1994 enabled those dispossessed since the Land Act of 1913 to reclaim their land but only with full compensation by the state to its present owners, few of whom were inclined to be cooperative. The government promised to focus on provision of housing and welfare, but the enormous backlog would take many years to overcome.

Although the inclusion of Inkatha in the government of national unity did lead to a drop in levels of violence, there was still much tension between IFP and ANC rivals in KwaZulu-Natal. There were signs in mid-1994 that the Zulu king, Goodwill Zwelithini, was less inclined to follow Buthelezi's lead than before the election and that Inkatha's localized power base might be weakened as a result. Indeed, none of the provinces were able to act effectively in the first year of their existence: they lacked funding and their powers remained vague and ill-defined.

Thus, the euphoria over the creation of a 'New South Africa' was primarily based on its remarkable political settlement rather than social or economic transformations. The legacy of apartheid will still lie heavily over the country in the late 1990s as it faces major problems of unemployment, urban migration and population growth. How far this will affect the popularity of the new government and of the ANC remains to be tested.

Cobbett, W. and Cohen, R. (eds) 1988: *Popular struggles in South Africa.* London: James Currey.

Frankel, P., Pines, N. and Swilling, M. (eds) 1988: *State, resistance and change in South Africa.* Johannesburg: Southern Books.

Friedman, S. and Atkinson D. 1994: *South African Review 7: The small miracle: South Africa's negotiated settlement.* Johannesburg: Ravan.

Lodge, T. and Nasson, B. 1991: *All, here, and now: black politics in South Africa in the 1980s.* Cape Town: Ford Foundation and David Philip.

Reynolds, A. (ed.) 1994: *Election '94 South Africa: the campaigns, results and future prospects.* London: James Currey and Cape Town: David Philip.

Bibliography

General Surveys

Davenport, R. 1991: *South Africa: a modern history*. 4th edn, London: Macmillan. (The most authoritative recent work.)

Pampallis, J. 1991: *Foundations of the new South Africa*. Cape Town: Maskew Miller Longman. (The ANC interpetation of the South African past.)

Shillington, K. 1987: *History of Southern Africa*. London: Longman. (Intended for school students.)

Stadler, A. 1987: *The political economy of modern South Africa*. London: Croom Helm; Cape Town: David Philip. (A thematic survey of twentieth-century developments.)

Thompson, L. 1990: *A history of South Africa*. New Haven: Yale University Press; Johannesburg: Random Century. (An interpretative overview.)

Sources Cited in Main Text

Alexander, N. 1991: 'Black consciousness: a reactionary tendency?' In N. Pityana, M. Ramphele, M. Mpumlwana and L. Wilson (eds) *Bounds of possibility: the legacy of Steve Biko and Black Consciousness*, London: Zed Books; Cape Town: David Philip, 238–56.

Atmore, A. and Marks, S. 1974: 'The imperial factor in South Africa in the nineteenth century: towards a reassessment'. *Journal of Imperial and Commonwealth History*, 3, 105–39.

Ballard C. 1989: 'Traders, trekkers and colonists'. In A. Duminy and B. Guest (eds) *Natal and Zululand from earliest times to 1910: a new history*,

Pietermaritzburg: University of Natal Press and Shuter and Shooter, 116–45.

Beinart, W. 1982: *The political economy of Pondoland, 1860 to 1930*. Cambridge: Cambridge University Press; Johannesburg: Ravan.

Beinart, W. 1987: 'Worker consciousness, ethnic particularism and nationalism: the experiences of a South African migrant, 1930–1960'. In S. Marks and S. Trapido (eds) *The politics of race, class and nationalism in twentieth century South Africa*, London: Longman, 286–309.

Beinart, W. and Bundy, C. 1987: *Hidden struggles in rural South Africa: politics and popular movements in the Transkei and Eastern Cape, 1890–1930*. Johannesburg: Ravan.

Biko, S. 1978: *I write what I like*. London: Heinemann.

Blainey, G. 1965: 'Lost causes of the Jameson Raid'. *Economic History Review*, 18, 350–66.

Bonner, P. 1982: 'The Transvaal Native Congress, 1917–1920: the radicalisation of the black petty bourgeoisie on the Rand'. In S. Marks and R. Rathbone (eds) *Industrialisation and social change in South Africa*, London: Longman, 270–313.

Bonner, P. 1983: *Kings, commoners and concessionaires: the evolution and dissolution of the nineteenth-century Swazi state*. Johannesburg: Ravan.

Bonner, P. 1990a: ' "Desirable or undesirable Sotho women?": liquor, prostitution and the migration of Basotho women to the Rand, 1920–1945'. In C. Walker (ed.) *Women and gender in Southern Africa to 1945*. London: James Currey; Cape Town: David Philip, 221–50.

Bonner, P. 1990b: 'The politics of black squatter movements on the Rand, 1944–1952'. *Radical History Review*, 46/7, 89–116.

Bonner, P. and Lambert, R. 1987: 'Batons and bare heads: the strike at Amato Textiles, February 1958'. In S. Marks and S. Trapido (eds) *The politics of race, class and nationalism in twentieth century South Africa*, London: Longman, 336–65.

Bradford, H. 1984: 'Mass movements and the petty bourgeoisie: the social origins of ICU leadership, 1924–29'. *Journal of African History*, 25, 295–310.

Bradford, H. 1987: *A taste of freedom: the ICU in rural South Africa, 1924–1930*. New Haven: Yale University Press; Johannesburg: Ravan.

Bradlow, E. 1989: 'The "Great Fear" at the Cape of Good Hope, 1851–52'. *International Journal of African Historical Studies*, 22, 401–21.

Bundy, C. 1972: 'The emergence and decline of a South African peasantry'. *African Affairs*, 71, 369–88.

Bundy, C. 1979: *The rise and fall of the South African peasantry*. London: Heinemann. 2nd edn, 1988, London: James Currey; Cape Town: David Philip.

Bundy, C. 1986: 'Vagabond Hollanders and runaway Englishmen: white poverty in the Cape before Poor Whiteism'. In W. Beinart, P. Delius and

S. Trapido (eds) *Putting a plough to the ground: accumulation and dispossession in rural South Africa, 1850–1930*. London: James Currey; Johannesburg: Ravan, 101–28.

Bundy, C. 1987a: 'Land and liberation: popular rural protest and the national liberation movements in South Africa, 1920–1960'. In S. Marks and S. Trapido (eds) *The politics of race, class and nationalism in twentieth century South Africa*, London: Longman, 254–85.

Bundy, C. 1987b: 'Street sociology and pavement politics: aspects of youth and student resistance in Cape Town, 1985'. *Journal of Southern African Studies*, 13, 303–30

Buthelezi, S. 1991: 'The emergence of Black Consciousness: an historical appraisal'. In N. Pityana, M. Ramphele, M. Mpumlwana and L. Wilson (eds) *Bounds of possibility: the legacy of Steve Biko and Black Consciousness*, London: Zed Books; Cape Town: David Philip, 111–29.

Campbell, C. 1992: 'Learning to kill? Masculinity, the family and violence in Natal'. *Journal of Southern African Studies*, 18, 614–28.

Carter, C. 1991: ' "We are the Progressives": Alexandra Youth Congress activists and the Freedom Charter, 1983–85'. *Journal of Southern African Studies*, 17, 197–220.

Cell, J. 1982: *The highest stage of White supremacy: the origins of segregation in South Africa and the American South*. Cambridge: Cambridge University Press.

Chaskalson, M. 1988: 'Rural resistance in the 1940s and 1950s'. *Africa Perspective*, 2, 47–57.

Chisholm, L. 1984: 'Redefining skills: black education in South Africa in the 1980s'. In P. Kallaway (ed.) *Apartheid and education: the education of black South Africans*, Johannesburg: Ravan, 387–409.

Christie, P. and Collins, C. 1984: 'Bantu education: apartheid ideology and labour reproduction'. In P. Kallaway (ed.) *Apartheid and education: the education of black South Africans*, Johannesburg: Ravan, 160–83.

Cobbett, W., Glaser, D., Hindson, D. and Swilling, M. 1988: 'A critical analysis of the South African state's reform strategies in the 1980s'. In P. Frankel, N. Pines and M. Swilling (eds) *State, resistance and change in South Africa*, Johannesburg: Southern Books, 19–51.

Cobbing, J. 1988: 'The Mfecane as alibi: thoughts on Dithakong and Mbolombo'. *Journal of African History*, 29, 487–519.

Cope, R.L. 1986: 'Strategic and socio-economic explanations for Carnarvon's South African confederation policy: the historiography and the evidence'. *History in Africa*, 13, 13–34.

Cope, R.L. 1989: 'C.W. de Kiewiet, the imperial factor and South African "Native Policy" '. *Journal of Southern African Studies*, 15, 486–505.

Coplan, D.B. 1985: *In township tonight!: South Africa's black city music and theatre*. Johannesburg: Ravan.

Crais, C.C. 1986: 'Gentry and labour in three Eastern Cape districts'. *South African Historical Journal*, 18, 125–46.

Davenport, R. 1987: 'The Cape liberal tradition to 1910'. In J. Butler, R. Elphick and D. Welsh (eds) *Democratic liberalism in South Africa: its history and prospect*. Middletown: Wesleyan University Press; Cape Town: David Philip, 21–34.

Davenport, R. 1991: *South Africa: a modern history*. 4th edn, London: Macmillan.

Davies, R. 1976: 'Mining capital, the state and unskilled white workers in South Africa, 1901–1913'. *Journal of Southern African Studies*, 3, 41–69.

Davies, R. 1979: *Capital, state and white labour in South Africa 1900–1960: an historical materialist analysis of class formation and class relations*. Brighton: Harvester Press.

Davies, R. and O'Meara, D. 1984: 'The state of analysis of the Southern African region: issues raised by South African strategy'. *Review of African Political Economy*, 29, 64–76.

Davies, R., Kaplan, D., Morris, M. and O'Meara, D. 1976: 'Class struggle and the periodisation of the state in South Africa'. *Review of African Political Economy*, 7, 4–30

Davies, R., O'Meara, D. and Dlamini, S. 1988: *The struggle for South Africa: a reference guide*. 2 vols, 2nd edn, London: Zed Books.

Davis, D. and Fine, R. 1985: 'Political strategies and the state: some historical observations'. *Journal of Southern African Studies*, 12, 25–48.

De Kiewiet, C.W. 1937: *The imperial factor in South Africa*. Cambridge: Cambridge University Press.

Delius, P. 1980: 'Migrant labour and the Pedi, 1840–80'. In S. Marks and A. Atmore (eds) *Economy and society in pre-industrial South Africa*, London: Longman, 293–312.

Delius, P. 1983: *The land belongs to us: the Pedi polity, the Boers and the British in the nineteenth century Transvaal*. Johannesburg: Ravan.

Dubow, S. 1986: 'Holding "a just balance balance between black and white": the Native Affairs Department in South Africa c.1920–1933'. *Journal of Southern African Studies*, 12, 217–39.

Dubow, S. 1987: 'Race, civilisation and culture: the elaboration of segregationalist discourse in the inter-war years'. In S. Marks and S. Trapido (eds) *The politics of race, class and nationalism in twentieth century South Africa*, London: Longman, 71–94.

Dubow, S. 1989: *Racial segregation and the origins of apartheid in South Africa*. London: Macmillan.

Dubow, S. 1992: 'Afrikaner nationalism, apartheid and the conceptualisation of "race" '. *Journal of African History*, 33, 209–37.

Du Toit, A: 1983: 'No chosen people: the myth of the Calvinist origins of Afrikaner nationalism and racial ideology'. *American Historical Review*, 88, 920–52.

Edgar, R. 1982: 'The prophet motive: Enoch Mgijima, the Israelites and the background to the Bulhoek massacre'. *International Journal of African Historical Studies*, 15, 401–22.

Eiselen, W. 1948: 'The meaning of apartheid'. *Race Relations Journal*, 15, 69–86.

Eldredge, E. 1992: 'Sources of conflict in Southern Africa, ca.1800–30: the "Mfecane" reconsidered'. *Journal of African History*, 33, 1–35.

Elphick, R and Giliomee, H. 1989: 'The origins and entrenchment of European dominance at the Cape, 1652–c.1840'. In R. Elphick and H. Giliomee (eds) *The shaping of South African society*, 1652–1840. Cape Town: Maskew Miller Longman, 521–66.

Elphick, R. and Malherbe, V.C. 1989: 'The Khoisan to 1828'. In R. Elphick and H. Giliomee (eds), *The shaping of South African society, 1652–1840*, Cape Town: Maskew Miller Longman, 3–65.

Elphick, R. and Shell, R. 1989: 'Intergroup relations: Khoikhoi, settlers, slaves and free blacks, 1652–1795'. In R. Elphick and H. Giliomee (eds) *The shaping of South African society, 1652–1840*. Cape Town: Maskew Miller Longman, 184–239.

Etherington, N. 1979: 'Labour supply and the genesis of South African confederation in the 1870s'. *Journal of African History*, 20, 235–53.

Etherington, N. 1985: 'African economic experiments in colonial Natal, 1845–1880'. In B. Guest and J. Sellers (eds) *Enterprise and exploitation in a Victorian colony: aspects of the economic and social history of colonial Natal*, Pietermaritzburg: University of Natal Press, 265–86.

Etherington, N. 1989: 'The "Shepstone system", in the colony of Natal and beyond the borders'. In A. Duminy and B. Guest (eds) *Natal and Zululand: from earliest times to 1910*. Pietermaritzburg: Shuter and Shooter and University of Natal Press, 170–92.

Etherington, N. 1991: 'The Great Trek in relation to the Mfecane'. *South African Historical Journal*, 25, 3–21.

Etherington, N. 1992: 'Explaining the death throes of apartheid'. In N. Etherington (ed.) *Peace, politics and violence in the new South Africa*. London: Hans Zell Publishers, 102–20.

Evans, M. and Phillips, M. 1988: 'Intensifying civil war: the role of the South African Defence Force'. In P. Frankel, N. Pines and M. Swilling (eds) *State, resistance and change in South Africa*, Johannesburg: Southern Books, 117–45.

Feit, E. 1967: *African opposition in South Africa: the failure of passive resistance*. Stanford: Hoover Institution on War, Revolution and Peace.

Feit, E. 1971: *Urban revolt in South Africa 1960–1964: a case study*. Evanston: Northwestern University Press.

Fine, R and Davis, D. 1991: *Beyond apartheid: labour and liberation in South Africa*. Johannesburg: Ravan.

Frankel, P. 1988: 'Beyond apartheid: pathways for transition'. In P. Frankel, N. Pines and M. Swilling (eds) *State, resistance and change in South Africa*, Johannesburg: Southern Books, 278–305.

Friedman, S. 1986: 'Understanding reform'. *South African Institute of Race Relations Position Paper*, 14.

Freund, B. 1976: 'Race in the social structure of South Africa, 1652–1836'. *Race and Class*, 18, 53–67.

Freund, B. 1989: 'The social character of secondary industry in South Africa, 1915–1945'. In A. Mabin (ed.) *Organisation and economic change: Southern African Studies*, vol.5. Johannesburg: Ravan, 78–119.

Gerhart, G: 1978: *Black power in South Africa: the evolution of an ideology.* Berkeley: University of California Press.

Giliomee, H. 1983: 'Constructing Afrikaner nationalism'. *Journal of Asian and African Studies*, 18, 83–98.

Giliomee, H. 1985: 'The changing political function of the homelands'. In H. Giliomee and L. Schlemmer (eds) *Up against the fences: poverty, passes and privilege in South Africa*, Cape Town: David Philip, 39–56.

Giliomee, H. 1987: 'Western Cape farmers and the beginnings of Afrikaner nationalism, 1870–1915'. *Journal of Southern African Studies*. 14, 38–63.

Giliomee, H. 1989: 'The beginnings of Afrikaner ethnic consciousness'. In L. Vail (ed.) *The creation of tribalism in Southern Africa*. London: James Currey, 21–54.

Giliomee, H. 1992: 'The last trek? Afrikaners in the transition to democracy'. In N. Etherington (ed.) *Peace, politics and the new South Africa*. London: Hans Zell Publishers, 28–45.

Gluckman, M. 1960: 'The rise of the Zulu empire'. *Scientific American*, 202, April, 157–68.

Goldin, I. 1987: 'The reconstruction of Coloured identity in the Western Cape'. In S. Marks and S. Trapido (eds) *The politics of race, class and nationalism in twentieth century South Africa*, London: Longman, 156–81.

Goodfellow, C.F. 1966: *Great Britain and the 'South African Confederation'.* Oxford: University Press.

Greenberg, S. 1987: 'Ideological struggles within the South African state'. In S. Marks and S. Trapido (eds) *The politics of race, class and nationalism in twentieth century South Africa*, London: Longman, 389–418.

Guelke, L. 1989: 'Freehold farmers and frontier settlers, 1657–1780'. In R. Elphick and H. Giliomee (eds) *The shaping of South African society, 1652–1840*, Cape Town: Maskew Miller Longman, 66–108.

Guy, J. 1980: 'Ecological factors in the rise of Shaka and the Zulu kingdom'. In S. Marks and A. Atmore (eds) *Economy and society in pre-industrial South Africa*, London: Longman, 102–19.

Guy, J. 1982: 'The destruction and reconstruction of Zulu society'. In S. Marks and R. Rathbone (eds) *Industrialisation and social change in South Africa*. London: Longman, 167–94.

Gwala, N. 1989: 'Political violence and the struggle for control in Pietermaritzburg'. *Journal of Southern African Studies*, 15, 506–24.

Halisi, C. 1991: 'Biko and Black Consciousness philosophy: an interpretation'. In N. Pityana, M. Ramphele, M. Mpumlwana and L. Wilson (eds) *Bounds of possibility: the legacy of Steve Biko and Black Consciousness*, Cape Town: David Philip, 100–10.

Hall, M. 1987: *The changing past: farmers, kings and traders in Southern Africa, 200–1860*. London: James Currey; Cape Town: David Philip.

Hamilton, C. 1992: 'The character and objectives of Shaka: a reconsideration of the making of Shaka as "Mfecane" motor'. *Journal of African History*, 33, 37–63.

Harries, P. 1982: 'Kinship, ideology and the nature of pre-colonial labour migration: labour migration from the Delagoa Bay hinterland to South Africa, up to 1895'. In S. Marks and R. Rathbone (eds) *Industrialisation and social change in South Africa*, London: Longman, 142–66.

Harries, P. 1986: 'Capital, state and labour on the 19th century Witwatersrand: a reassessment'. *South African Historical Journal*, 18, 25–45.

Harries, P. 1987: 'Plantations, passes and proletarians: labour and the colonial state in nineteenth century Natal'. *Journal of Southern African Studies*, 13, 372–99.

Haysom, N. 1989: 'Vigilantes and militarisation of South Africa'. In J. Cock and L. Nathan (eds) *War and society: the militarisation of South Africa*, Cape Town: David Philip, 188–99.

Hellman, E. 1935: 'Native life in a Johannesburg slum yard'. *Africa*, 8, 34–62.

Hill, R. and Pirio, G. 1987: ' "Africa for the Africans": the Garvey movement in South Africa, 1920–1940'. In S. Marks and S. Trapido (eds) *The politics of race, class and nationalism in twentieth century South Africa*, London: Longman, 209–53.

Hindson, D. 1987: *Pass controls and the urban African proletariat*. Johannesburg: Ravan.

Hirson, B. 1979: *Year of fire, year of ash: the Soweto revolt: roots of a revolution?*. London: Zed Press.

Hofmeyr, I. 1987: 'Building a nation from words: Afrikaans language, literature and ethnic identity, 1902–1924'. In S. Marks and S. Trapido (eds) *The politics of race, class and nationalism in twentieth century South Africa*, London: Longman, 95–124.

Hudson, P. 1988: 'Images of the future and strategies in the present: the Freedom Charter and the South African Left'. In P. Frankel, N. Pines and M. Swilling (eds) *State, resistance and change in South Africa*, Johannesburg, Southern Books, 259–77.

Hughes, H. 1987: 'Violence in Inanda, August 1985'. *Journal of Southern African Studies*, 13, 331–54.

Hyam, R. 1972: *The failure of South African expansion, 1908–1948*. London: Macmillan.

Hyslop, J. 1988: 'School student movements and state education policy, 1972–87'. In W. Cobbett and R. Cohen (eds) *Popular struggles in South Africa*, London: James Currey, 183–209.

Jeeves, A. 1975: 'The control of migratory labour in the South African gold mines in the era of Kruger and Milner'. *Journal of Southern African Studies*, 2, 3–29.

Jeeves, A. 1985: *Migrant labour in South Africa's mining economy: the struggle for the gold mines' labour supply 1890–1920*. Johannesburg: Witwatersrand University Press.

Johnstone, F. 1976: *Class, race and gold: a study of class relations and racial discrimination in South Africa*. London: Routledge and Kegan Paul.

Karis, T. and Carter, G. 1973: *From protest to challenge: a documentary history of African politics in South Africa, 1882–1964*. 4 vols, Stanford: Hoover Press.

Keegan, T. 1982: 'The sharecropping economy, African class formation and the Natives' Land Act of 1913 in the highveld maize belt'. In S. Marks and R. Rathbone (eds) *Industrialisation and social change in South Africa*, London: Longman, 195–211.

Keegan, T. 1986: *Rural transformations in industrializing South Africa: the southern highveld to 1914*. London: Macmillan; Johannesburg: Ravan.

Kentridge, M. 1990: *An unofficial war: inside the conflict in Pietermaritzburg*. Cape Town: David Philip.

Kimble, J. 1982: 'Labour migration in Basutoland, c.1870–1885'. In S. Marks and R. Rathbone (eds) *Industrialisation and social change in South Africa*, London: Longman, 119–41.

Kinsman, M. 1983: 'Between two stones: the onset of migrant labour amongst the Southern Tswana'. *University of Cape Town: Africa Seminar. Collected Papers*, vol.3, 226–56.

Kirk, T. 1980: 'The Cape economy and the expropriation of the Kat River Settlement, 1846–53'. In S. Marks and A. Atmore (eds) *Economy and society in pre-industrial South Africa*, London: Longman, 226–46.

Koch, E. 1983: ' "Without visible means of subsistence": slumyard culture in Johannesburg 1918–1940'. In B. Bozzoli (ed.) *Town and countryside in the Transvaal: capitalist penetration and popular response*. Johannesburg: Ravan, 151–75.

Krikler, J. 1989: 'Agrarian class struggle and the South African War'. *Social History*, 14, 151–76.

Lacey, M. 1981: *Working for Boroko: the origins of a coercive labour system in South Africa*. Johannesburg: Ravan.

La Hausse, P. 1988: *Brewers, beerhalls and boycotts: a history of liquor in South Africa*. Johannesburg: Ravan.

Lambert, R. 1981: 'Black resistance in South Africa, 1950–1961: an assessment of the political strike campaigns'. *The societies of Southern Africa in the 19th and 20th centuries*, vol.10, Institute of Commonwealth Studies, University of London, 112–20.

Leatt, J., Kneifel, T. and Nurnberger, K. 1986: *Contending ideologies in South Africa*. Cape Town: David Philip.

Legassick, M. 1980: 'The frontier tradition in South African historiography'. In S. Marks and A. Atmore (eds) *Economy and society in pre-industrial South Africa*, London: Longman, 44–79.

Levy, N. 1982: *The foundations of the South African cheap labour system*. London: Routledge and Kegan Paul.

Lewis, G. 1987: *Between the wire and the wall: a history of South African 'Coloured' politics*. New York: St Martin's Press; Cape Town: David Philip.

Lewsen, P. 1971: 'The Cape liberal tradition – myth or reality?' *Race*, 13, 65–80.

Lewsen, P. 1983: 'Cape liberalism in its terminal phase'. In D. Hindson (ed.) *Working papers in Southern African Studies*, vol. 3, Johannesburg: Ravan, 33–50.

Lipton, M. 1988: 'Capitalism and apartheid'. In J. Lonsdale (ed.) *South Africa in question*. Cambridge University, African Studies Centre, 52–63.

Lodge, T. 1983: *Black politics in South Africa since 1945*. London: Longman and Johannesburg: Ravan.

Lodge, T. 1987: 'Political mobilisation during the 1950s: an East London case study'. In S. Marks and S. Trapido (eds) *The politics of race, class and nationalism in twentieth century South Africa*, London: Longman, 310–35.

Lodge, T. 1988: 'State of exile: the African National Congress of South Africa, 1976–1986'. In P. Frankel, N. Pines and M. Swilling (eds) *State, resistance and change in South Africa*, Johannesburg: Southern Books, 229–58.

Lodge, T. and Nasson, B. 1991: *All, here, and now: black politics in South Africa in the 1980s*. New York: Ford Foundation; Cape Town: David Philip.

Mabin, A. 1986: 'The rise and decline of Port Elizabeth, 1850–1900'. *International Journal of African Historical Studies*, 19, 275–303.

Mabin, A. 1992: 'Comprehensive segregation: the origins of the Group Areas Act and its planning apparatus'. *Journal of Southern African Studies*, 18, 405–29.

Maclennan, B. 1986: *A proper degree of terror: John Graham and the Cape's eastern frontier*. Johannesburg: Ravan.

Mafeje, A. 1978: 'Soweto and its aftermath'. *Review of African Political Economy*, 11, 17–30.

Mann, M. 1988: 'The giant stirs: South African business in the age of reform'. In P. Frankel, N. Pines and M. Swilling (eds) *State, resistance and change in South Africa*, Johannesburg: Southern Books, 52–86.

Marks, S. 1970: *Reluctant rebellion: the 1906–8 disturbances in Natal*. Oxford: Clarendon Press.

155

Marks, S. 1978: 'Natal, the Zulu royal family and the ideology of segregation'. *Journal of Southern African Studies*, 4, 172–94.

Marks, S. 1986a: *The ambiguities of dependence in South Africa: class, nationalism and the state in twentieth century Natal.* Johannesburg: Ravan.

Marks, S. 1986b: 'Class, ideology and the Bambatha rebellion'. In D. Crummey (ed.) *Banditry, rebellion and social protest in Africa.* London: James Currey, 351–72.

Marks, S. and Trapido, S. 1979: 'Lord Milner and the South African state'. *History Workshop Journal*, 2, 50–80.

Maylam, P. 1986: *A history of the African people of South Africa: from the early Iron Age to the 1970s.* Cape Town: David Philip.

Maylam, P. 1990: 'The rise and decline of urban apartheid in South Africa'. *African Affairs*, 89 (354), 57–84.

McCaul, C. 1988: 'The wild card: Inkatha and contemporary black politics'. In P. Frankel, N. Pines and M. Swilling (eds) *State, resistance and change in South Africa,* Johannesburg: Southern Books, 146–73.

Mendelsohn, R. 1980: 'Blainey and the Jameson Raid: the debate renewed'. *Journal of Southern African Studies*, 6, 157–70.

Moll, T. 1988: *No blade of grass: rural production and state intervention in Transkei, 1925–1960.* Cambridge African Occasional Papers, 6, Cambridge: African Studies Centre.

Molteno, F. 1977: 'The historical significance of the Bantustan strategy'. *Social Dynamics*, 3, 15–33.

Moroney, S. 1982: 'Mine married quarters: the differential stabilisation of the Witwatersrand workforce, 1900–1920'. In S. Marks and R. Rathbone (eds) *Industrialisation and social change in South Africa,* London: Longman, 259–69.

Morrell, R. 1986: 'Competition and cooperation in Middelburg, 1900–1930'. In W. Beinart, P. Delius and S. Trapido (eds) *Putting a plough to the ground: accumulation and dispossession in rural South Africa, 1850–1930.* London: James Currey; Johannesburg: Ravan, 373–419.

Morris, M. and Padayachee, V. 1988: 'State reform policy in South Africa'. *Transformation*, 7, 1–26.

Moss, G. 1980: ' "Total strategy" '. *Work in Progress*, 11, 1–11.

Muller, C. 1975: *Five hundred years: a history of South Africa.* 2nd edn, Pretoria and Cape Town: Academica.

Murray, M. 1987: *South Africa: time of agony, time of destiny: the upsurge of popular protest.* London: Verso.

Nasson, W. 1983: ' "Doing down their masters": Africans, Boers and treason in the Cape Colony, 1899–1902'. *Journal of Imperial and Commonwealth History*, 12, 29–53.

Nasson, W. 1989: ' "She preferred living in a cave with Harry the snake-catcher": towards an oral history of popular leisure and class expression in District Six, Cape Town, *c.* 1920–1950'. In P. Bonner, I. Hofmeyr, D.

James and T. Lodge (eds) *Holding their ground: class, locality and culture in 19th and 20th century South Africa*. Johannesburg: Ravan and Witwatersrand University Press, 285–309.

Nasson, W. 1990: 'The Unity Movement: its legacy in historical consciousness'. *Radical History Review* 46–7, 189–211.

Nasson, W. 1991: *Abraham Esau's war: a black South African war in the Cape, 1899–1902*. Cambridge: Cambridge University Press; Cape Town: David Philip.

Nathan, L. 1989: ' "Marching to a different beat": the history of the End Conscription Campaign'. In J. Cock and L. Nathan (eds) *War and society: the militarisation of South Africa*, Cape Town: David Philip, 308–23.

Newton-King, S. 1987: 'Commerce and material culture on the Eastern Cape frontier, 1784–1812'. Unpublished paper, History Workshop Conference, 'The Making of Class', Johannesburg, February 1987.

Newton-King, S. and Malherbe, C. 1981: *The Khoikhoi rebellion in the E.Cape (1799–1803)*. Cape Town: University of Cape Town, Centre for African Studies, Communications No. 5.

Odendaal, A. 1984: *Vukani Bantu!: the beginnings of black protest politics in South Africa to 1912*. Cape Town: David Philip.

O'Meara, D. 1976: 'The 1946 African mineworkers' strike in the political economy of South Africa'. *Journal of Commonwealth and Comparative Politics*, 13, 146–73.

O'Meara, D. 1978: 'Analysing Afrikaner nationalism: the "Christian-National" assault on white trade unionism in South Africa, 1934–1948'. *African Affairs*, 77, 45–72.

O'Meara, D. 1983: *Volkskapitalisme: class, capital and ideology in the development of Afrikaner nationalism, 1934–1948*. Cambridge: Cambridge University Press; Johannesburg: Ravan.

Omer-Cooper, J. 1966: *The Zulu aftermath: a nineteenth-century revolution in Bantu Africa*. London: Longman.

Pampallis, J. 1991: *Foundations of the new South Africa*. Cape Town: Maskew Miller Longman.

Peires, J. 1981: *The House of Phalo: a history of the Xhosa people in the days of their independence*. Johannesburg: Ravan Press.

Peires, J. 1986: ' "Soft" believers and "hard" unbelievers in the Xhosa cattle-killing'. *Journal of African History*, 27, 443–61.

Peires, J. 1987: 'The central beliefs of the Xhosa cattle-killing. *Journal of African History*, 28, 43–63.

Peires, J. 1989: 'The British and the Cape, 1814–1834'. In R. Elphick and H. Giliomee (eds) *The shaping of South African society, 1652–1840*, Cape Town: Maskew Miller Longman, 472–518.

Penn, N. 1989: 'Land, labour and livestock in the Western Cape during the eighteenth century'. In W.G. James and M. Simons (eds) *The angry divide: social and economic history of the Western Cape*. Cape Town: David Philip.

Plaatje, S. 1916: *Native life in South Africa*. Reprinted in 1982, Johannesburg: Ravan.

Platzky, L. and Walker C. 1985: *The surplus people: forced removals in South Africa*. Johannesurg: Ravan.

Porter, A. 1990: 'The South African War (1899–1902): context and motive reconsidered'. *Journal of African History*, 31, 43–57.

Posel, D. 1984: ' "Providing for the legitimate labour requirements of employers": secondary industry, commerce and the state in South Africa during the 1950s and 1960s'. Unpublished African Studies Institute seminar paper, University of the Witwatersrand, 29 October 1984.

Posel, D. 1987: 'The meaning of apartheid before 1948: conflicting interests and forces within the Afrikaner Nationalist alliance'. *Journal of Southern African Studies*, 14, 123–39.

Posel, D. 1988: 'The construction of apartheid, 1948–61'. Unpublished African Studies Institute seminar paper, University of the Witwatersrand, 22 August 1988.

Posel, D. 1990: 'The state and policy-making in apartheid's second phase'. History Workshop Conference, 'Structure and experience in the making of apartheid'. University of the Witwatersrand, February 1990.

Posel, D. 1991: *The making of apartheid 1948–1961: conflict and compromise*. Oxford: Clarendon Press.

Rich, P. 1978: 'Ministering to the white man's needs: the development of urban segregation in South Africa 1913–1923'. *African Studies*, 37, 177–91.

Rich, P. 1980: 'The origins of apartheid ideology: the case of Ernest Stubbs and the Transvaal Native Administration, 1902–1932'. *African Affairs*, 35, 229–51.

Rich, P. 1981: 'Segregation and the Cape liberal tradition'. *The societies of Southern Africa in the 19th and 20th centuries*, vol. 10, Institute of Commonwealth Studies, University of London, 31–40.

Rich, P. 1984: *White power and the liberal conscience: racial segregation and South African liberalism*. Johannesburg: Ravan.

Richardson, P. 1982: *Chinese mine labour in the Transvaal*. London: Macmillan.

Richardson, P. 1986: 'The Natal sugar industry in the nineteenth century'. In W. Beinart, P. Delius and S. Trapido (eds) *Putting a plough to the ground: accumulation and dispossession in rural South Africa, 1850–1930*, Johannesburg: Ravan, 129–75.

Richardson, P. and Van-Helten, J.J. 1980: 'The gold mining industry in the Transvaal, 1886–99'. In P. Warwick (ed.) *The South African War: the Anglo–Boer War, 1899–1902*. London: Longman, 18–36.

Richardson, P. and Van-Helten, J.J. 1982: 'Labour in the South African gold mining industry'. In S. Marks and R. Rathbone (eds) *Industrialisation and social change in South Africa*, London: Longman, 77–98.

Ritner, S. 1967: 'The Dutch Reformed Church and apartheid'. *Journal of Contemporary History*, 2, 17–37.

Robinson, R. and Gallagher, J. 1961: *Africa and the Victorians: the official mind of imperialism*. London: Macmillan.

Ross, R. 1975: 'The "white" population of South Africa in the eighteenth century'. *Population Studies*. 29, 217–30.

Ross, R. 1986: 'The origins of capitalist agriculture in the Cape Colony: a survey'. In W. Beinart, P. Delius and S. Trapido (eds) *Putting a plough to the ground: accumulation and dispossession in rural South Africa, 1850–1930*, Johannesburg: Ravan, 56–100.

Ross, R. 1989: 'The Cape of Good Hope and the world economy, 1652–1835'. In R. Elphick and H. Giliomee (eds) *The shaping of South African society, 1652–1840*, Cape Town: Maskew Miller Longman, 243–82.

Sapire, H. 1987: 'The stay-away of the Brakpan location, 1944'. In B. Bozzoli (ed.) *Class, community and conflict: South African perspectives*, Johannesburg: Ravan, 358–400.

Sapire, H. 1989a: 'African political mobilisation in Brakpan in the 1950s'. Unpublished African Studies Institute seminar paper, University of the Witwatersrand, 20 March 1989.

Sapire, H. 1989b: 'African settlement and segregation in Brakpan, 1900–1927'. In P. Bonner, I. Hofmeyr, D. James and T. Lodge (eds) *Holding their ground: class, locality and culture in 19th and 20th century South Africa*, Johannesburg: Ravan and Witwatersrand University Press, 141–76.

Sapire, H. 1992: 'Politics and protest in shack settlements of the Pretoria–Witwatersrand–Vereeniging region, South Africa, 1980–1990'. *Journal of Southern African Studies*, 18, 670–97.

Saunders, C. 1970: 'The new African elite in the eastern Cape and some late nineteenth century origins of African nationalism'. *The societies of Southern Africa in the 19th and 20th centuries*, vol.1, Institute of Commonwealth Studies, University of London, 44–55.

Saunders, C. 1988: *The making of the South African past: major historians on race and class*. Totowa: Barnes and Noble; Cape Town: David Philip.

Saunders, C. 1992: *Writing history: South Africa's urban past and other essays*. Pretoria: Human Sciences Research Council.

Seekings, J. 1988: 'Political mobilisation in the black townships of the Transvaal'. In P. Frankel, N. Pines and M. Swilling (eds) *State, resistance and change in South Africa*, Johannesburg: Southern Books, 197–228.

Segal, L. 1992: 'The human face of violence: hostel dwellers speak'. *Journal of Southern African Studies*, 18, 190–231.

Shillington, K. 1982: 'The impact of the diamond discoveries on the Kimberley hinterland: class formation, colonialism and resistance among the Thlaping of Griqualand West in the 1870s'. In S. Marks and R. Rathbone (eds) *Industrialisation and social change in South Africa*, London: Longman, 99–118.

Shillington, K. 1985: *The colonisation of the Southern Tswana, 1870–1900.* Johannesburg: Ravan.

Sitas, A. 1992: 'The making of the "Comrades" movement in Natal, 1985– 91'. *Journal of Southern African Studies,* 18, 629–41.

Slater, H. 1975: 'Land, labour and capital in Natal: the Natal Land and Colonisation Company, 1860–1948'. *Journal of African History,* 16, 257–83.

Slater, H. 1980: 'The changing pattern of economic relationships in rural Natal, 1838–1914'. In S. Marks and A. Atmore (eds) *Economy and society in pre-industrial South Africa,* London: Longman, 148–70.

Smith, A. 1969: 'The trade of Delagoa Bay as a factor in Nguni politics 1750–1835'. In L. Thompson (ed.) *African Societies in Southern Africa.* London: Heinemann, 171–89.

Smith, I. 1988: 'The revolution in South African historiography'. *History Today,* 38, February, 8–10.

Smith, I. 1990: 'The origins of the South African War (1899–1902): a reappraisal'. *South African Historical Journal,* 22, 24–60.

Southall, R. 1981: 'Buthelezi, Inkatha and the politics of compromise'. *African Affairs,* 80, 453–81.

Southall, R. 1982: *South Africa's Transkei: the political economy of an 'independent' Bantustan.* London: Heinemann.

Stadler, A. 1979: 'Birds in the cornfield: squatter movements in Johannesburg, 1944–1947'. *Journal of Southern African Studies,* 6, 93–123.

Stadler, A. 1981: 'A long way to walk: bus boycotts in Alexandria, 1940– 1945'. In P. Bonner (ed.) *Working Papers in Southern African Studies,* vol.2. Johannesburg: Ravan, 228–57.

Stadler, A. 1987: *The political economy of modern South Africa.* London: Croom Helm; Cape Town: David Philip.

Swan, M. 1987: 'Ideology in organised Indian politics, 1891–1948'. In S. Marks and S. Trapido (eds) *The politics of race, class and nationalism in twentieth century South Africa,* London: Longman, 182–208.

Swanson, M. 1976: ' "The Durban system": roots of urban segregation in colonial Natal'. *African Studies,* 35, 159–76.

Swanson, M. 1977: 'The sanitation syndrome: bubonic plague and urban native policy in the Cape Colony, 1900–1909'. *Journal of African History,* 18, 387–410.

Swanson, M. 1983: ' "The Asiatic menace": creating segregation in Durban, 1870–1900'. *International Journal of African Historical Studies,* 16, 401–21.

Swilling, M. 1988: 'The United Democratic Front and township revolt'. In W. Cobbett and R. Cohen (eds) *Popular struggles in South Africa,* London: James Currey, 90–113.

Swilling, M. and Phillips, M. 1989: 'State power in the 1980s: from "total strategy" to counter-revolutionary warfare'. In J. Cock and L. Nathan (eds) *War and society: the militarisation of South Africa,* Cape Town: David Philip, 134–148.

Terreblanche, S. and Nattrass, N. 1990: 'A periodization of the political economy'. In N. Nattrass and E. Ardington (eds) *The political economy of South Africa*, Cape Town: Oxford University Press, 6–23.

Transvaal Rural Action Committee 1988: 'Kwandebele – the struggle against "independence" '. In W. Cobbett and R. Cohen (eds) *Popular struggles in South Africa*, London: James Currey, 114–35.

Trapido, S. 1970: 'South Africa in a comparative study of industrialisation'. *Journal of Development Studies*, 7, 309–20.

Trapido, S. 1978: 'Landlord and tenant in a colonial economy: the Transvaal, 1880–1910'. *Journal of Southern African Studies*, 5, 26–58.

Trapido, S. 1980: ' "The friends of the natives": merchants, peasants and the political and ideological structure of liberalism at the Cape'. In S. Marks and A. Atmore (eds) *Economy and society in pre-industrial South Africa*, London: Longman, 247–74.

Trapido, S. 1986: 'Putting a plough to the ground: a history of tenant production on the Vereeniging estates, 1896–1920'. In W. Beinart, P. Delius and S. Trapido (eds) *Putting a plough to the ground: accumulation and dispossession in rural South Africa, 1850–1930*. Johannesburg: Ravan, 336–72.

Turrell, R. 1982: 'Kimberley: labour and compounds, 1871–1888'. In S. Marks and R. Rathbone (eds) *Industrialisation and social change in South Africa*, London: Longman, 45–76.

Turrell, R. 1984: 'Kimberley's model compounds'. *Journal of African History*, 25, 59–76.

Turrell, R. 1987: *Capital and labour on the Kimberley diamond fields, 1871–1890*. Cambridge: Cambridge University Press.

Vail, L. 1989: 'Ethnicity in Southern African history'. In L. Vail (ed.) *The creation of tribalism in Southern Africa*. London: James Currey.

Van Onselen, C. 1972: 'Reactions to rinderpest in Southern Africa, 1896–97'. *Journal of African History*, 13, 473–88.

Van Onselen, C. 1982: *Studies in the social and economic history of the Witwatersrand 1886–1914*. vol.I: *New Babylon*, vol.II: *New Nineveh*. Longman: London; Johannesburg: Ravan.

Wagner, R. 1980: 'Zoutpansberg: the dynamics of a hunting frontier, 1848–67'. In S. Marks and A. Atmore (eds) *Economy and society in pre-industrial South Africa*, London: Longman, 313–49.

Walker, C. (ed.) 1990: *Women and gender in Southern Africa to 1945*. Cape Town: David Philip; London: James Currey.

Warwick, P. (ed.) 1980: 'The South African War: the Anglo–Boer War, 1899–1902'. London: Longman.

Warwick, P. 1983: *Black people and the South African War, 1899–1902*. London: Longman; Johannesburg: Ravan.

Webster, E. 1977: 'The 1946 [sic] Durban "riots": a case study in race and class'. In P. Bonner (ed.) *Working papers in Southern African studies*.

Johannesburg: African Studies Institute, University of the Witwatersrand, 1–54.

Webster, E. 1988: 'The rise of social-movement unionism: the two faces of the black trade union movement in South Africa'. In P. Frankel, N. Pines and M. Swilling (eds) *State, resistance and change in South Africa*, Johannesburg: Southern Books, 174–96.

Welsh, D. 1971: *The roots of segregation: native policy in colonial Natal, 1845–1910*. Cape Town: Oxford University Press.

Wickens, P. 1978: *The Industrial and Commercial Workers' Union of Africa*. Cape Town: Oxford University Press.

Willan, B. 1978: 'Sol Plaatje, De Beers and an old tram shed: class relations and social control in a South African town, 1918–19'. *Journal of Southern African Studies*, 4, 195–215.

Williams, G. 1988: 'Celebrating the Freedom Charter'. *Transformation*, 6, 73–86.

Wilson, F. 1971: 'Farming, 1866–1966'. In M. Wilson and L. Thompson (eds) *The Oxford History of South Africa*, vol. II, Oxford: Oxford University Press, 104–71.

Wilson, F and Ramphele, M. 1989: *Uprooting poverty: the South African challenge*. New York: W W Norton; Cape Town: David Philip.

Wilson, M. and Thompson, L. 1971: *The Oxford History of South Africa*. 2 vols, Oxford: Oxford University Press.

Wolpe, H. 1972: 'Capitalism and cheap labour power in South Africa: from segregation to apartheid'. *Economy and Society*, 1, 425–56.

Wolpe, H. 1988: *Race, class and the apartheid state*. London: James Currey.

Worden, N. 1985: *Slavery in Dutch South Africa*. Cambridge: Cambridge University Press.

Worden, N. 1989: 'Adjusting to emancipation: freed slaves and farmers in the mid-nineteenth century south-western Cape. In W. James and M. Simons (eds) *The angry divide: social and economic history of the western Cape*. Cape Town: David Philip, 31–9.

Worden, N. and Crais, C. (eds) 1994: *Breaking the chains: slavery and its legacy in the nineteenth century Cape Colony*. Johannesburg: Witwatersrand University Press.

Worger, W. 1987: *South Africa's city of diamonds: mine workers and monopoly capitalism in Kimberley, 1867–1895*. New Haven: Yale University Press.

Index

Abdurahman, Abdullah, 84
Abolition of Passes and
   Coordination of Documents
   Act (1952), 98
Accra conference (1958), 106
Africanist, The, 106
African National Congress (ANC),
   57, 60; foundation of and pre-
   1940s, 81–3, 85–7; in 1950s,
   100, 102–4; banned (1960),
   107, 108; after banning,
   114–16; and Black
   Consciousness, 116–17; and
   Soweto, 119; in 1980s, 130–1;
   unbanning (1990), 137;
   conflict with Inkatha, 139; in
   1994 election, 143–4; *see also*
   Defiance Campaign, Transvaal
   Native Congress, Youth
   League
African nationalism, 79–87
African People's Organisation
   (APO), 84, 85; *see also* South
   African Coloured People's
   Organisation
African Resistance Movement, 114,
   115
Afrikaanse Handelsinstituut, 109,
   123
Afrikaanse Patriot, Die, 88

Afrikaans language, 88, 90, 119
Afrikaner Bond, 88
Afrikaner nationalism, 24, 87–94,
   122, 123
Afrikaner rebellion (1914), 87, 90
Afrikaner Weerstand Beweging
   (AWB), 141, 143
Aggett, Neil, 127
Alexandra, 63, 101, 103, 130
All African Convention (AAC), 85
Anglo American Corporation, 38
Angola, 115, 119–20, 122, 125,
   138
apartheid: formulation of, 92–3;
   implemention of, 95–9,
   108–13; reform of, 121–5,
   137; *see also* Separate
   Development
Atlantic Charter (1941), 86
Azanian Confederation of Trade
   Unions (AZACTU), 127
Azanian People's Liberation Army
   (APLA), 141
Azanian People's Organisation
   (AZAPO), 128, 130; banned,
   131, 141, 145

Bambatha rebellion (1906–8), 23,
   32
Bantu Affairs Department, 108–9

163

Bantu Authorities Act (1951), 96,
  99–100, 102, 110
Bantu Education Act (1953), 96;
  resistance to, 100
Bantu Labour Act (1964), 109
Bantustans, 110–13, 114, 135
Basutoland, see Lesotho
Beaumont Commission (1916), 60
Bechuanaland, see Botswana
Benoni, 52; and Defiance
  Campaign, 103–4
Biko, Steve, 116, 117, 118
Bill of Rights (1994), 142
Bisho, 140
Black Communities Project, 116
Black Consciousness, 86, 116–18,
  127, 128, 131, 133; and
  Soweto, 119
Black Flag revolt (1875), 38
Black Local Authorities Act (1982),
  125
Black People's Convention (BPC),
  116
Black Peril slogan (1929), 77, 83
Bloemfontein, 29, 32
Bloemfontein Convention (1854),
  16
Boer War, see South African War
Boipatong, 139–40
Bophutatswana, 111, 112; member
  of COSAG, 140;
  reincorporation, 143
Botha, Louis, 73
Botha, 'Pik', 135
Botha, P. W., 122, 125, 135, 136
Botswana, 21, 32, 125, 136
Brakpan: segregation in, 44;
  stayaway (1944), 63; Defiance
  Campaign, 104
Broederbond, Afrikaner, 89, 90,
  91, 93, 108–9
Brooks, Edgar, 78
Bulhoek massacre (1921), 55
Burger, De, 89

Buthelezi, Mangosutho, 118, 133,
  139, 140, 143, 144, 145

Caledon Code (1809), 68
Cape Colony: foundation, 8;
  expansion, 23–4; land control,
  48, 60; franchise, 68, 69–70,
  75; see also liberalism
Cape Town, 11, 32, 35, 61; racial
  structure, 66–7, 68;
  segregation and forced
  removals, 42, 69, 96;
  dockworker strike (1919), 53;
  disturbances (1976), 119;
  African urbanization, 126;
  meat workers strike (1980),
  127; see also Crossroads,
  District Six, Hout Bay,
  Khayelitsha, Langa
Cape, Western: in 1994 election,
  144
Carlton Conference (1979), 123
Carnarvon, federation scheme,
  20–1
Carnegie Commission (1932), 59
Cato Manor, 62, 101, 108
Cetshwayo, 23
Charterism, 105–6, 127, 128, 130
Christian National education, 89,
  90
churches, African independent, 54,
  81, 106
Cillie Commission (1976), 119
Ciskei: conquest, 17–18, 69;
  peasant farming, 46;
  landlessness, 59; Bantustan,
  110, 111, 112; march on
  (1992), 140; member of
  COSAG, 140; reincorporation,
  143
civilized labour policy, 74
coloured people: and Black
  Consciousness, 117;
  classification, 68; political

organization, 84; segregation of, 96; *see also* franchise
Commonwealth, British: South Africa leaves (1961), 107; delegation and sanctions (1986), 135
Communist Party of South Africa, 53, 83, 85, 86, 104, 105, 106; unbanning, 137, 138
Community Councils, 124–5, 129
Concerned South Africans Group (COSAG), 140
Congress of Democrats, 104, 105
Congress of South African Trade Unions (COSATU), 127
Conservative Party, 122, 136, 138, 140–2
Constitution, interim (1994), 141–2
Convention for a Democratic South Africa (CODESA), 137, 139, 140
Council for Non-European Trade Unions (CNETU), 64
Cresswell, F. S., 51, 74
Criminal Law Amendment Act (1953), 97, 100
Crossroads, 126, 132

de Beers Consolidated Mines Company, 38, 83
Defiance Campaign (1952), 100
de Klerk, F. W., 136–44
de Lange Report (1981), 124
Democratic Party, 136, 143, 144
Department of Co-operation and Development, 126
Depression, Great (1930–3), 57–9
diamond mining, 19, 37–9
Dingane, 15
District Six, 62, 63
Doornfontein, 62
Dube, John, 80, 82
Durban, 14, 42, 61; segregation in, 42–3; conflict (1949), 104–5, 132; strikes (1970s), 118;

UDF and Inkatha support in, 133; *see also* Cato Manor, Durban 'system', Inanda, KwaMashu, Umlazi
Durban 'system', 43, 62
Dutch East India Company (VOC), 7–8, 66
Dutch Reformed Church, 59, 70, 88, 89

East London, 61, 80, 100; and Defiance Campaign, 103; strikes (1970s), 118
Eeufees, 91
Eiselen, W. M. M., 93, 98
election (1994), 143–4
Emergency, State of (1960), 107; (1980s), 130, 131, 136; (1994), 143
End Conscription Campaign (ECC), 132
ethnicity, 76–8, 82, 112, 133

Fagan Commission (1946), 92
Federasie van Afrikaanse Kultuurverenigings (FAK), 89, 90, 93
flag, 90
forced removals, 42, 96, 111
franchise, pre-Union, 68–70; of Africans, 71, 124; Cape African franchise, 68, 75, 83; of coloured people, 68, 84, 97, 124; of Indians, 70, 96, 124
Freedom Charter (1955), 105–6, 143
Freedom Front (FF), 142, 144
Free State, *see* Orange Free State
Fusion government, 58, 90

Gandhi, Mahatma, 84–5
Garveyism, 55, 83
General Law Amendment Act (1963), 108

Genootskap van Regte Afrikaners, 88
Germiston, 52
Ghetto Act (1946), 86
Glen Grey Act (1894), 48, 54, 69
Godley Committee (1919), 43
gold mining, 39–40, 99; and South African War, 26–8
Goldstone Commission (1992), 140
Gool, Cissie, 85
Gorbachev 'revolution', 138
Gqozo, Oupa, 143
Great Trek, 12–13, 70; see also Eeufees
Griqua, 16, 21
Griqualand West, 21, 25, 38
Group Areas Act (1950), 96; repealed, 137
Gumede, Josiah, 83

Hani, Chris, 141
Herenigde Nasionale Party, see National Party
Herschel district, 54
Hertzog, J. B., 76, 78, 91; see also National Party
Hintsa, 12
historiography of South Africa, 2–3; of segregation, 66
homelands, see Bantustans
Hout Bay, 62
Huisgenoot, Die, 89

Ilanga lase Natal, 80
Imbumba ya Manyama, 80
Immorality Act (1950), 95; abolition of, 124
Imvo Zabantsundu, 80
Inanda, 132
indentured labour: from India, 15, 36, 46; from China, 30, 41, 46
independent churches, see churches
India, independence and sanctions against South Africa, 86
Indian Congress, 85, 86, 105

Indians, indentured workers, 15, 36, 46; early political organization, 84–5; segregation of, 93, 96; 1949 conflicts and status of, 105; and Black Consciousness, 117; see also franchise, Ghetto Act, Indian Congress
Industrial and Commercial Workers' Union (ICU), 53, 55–7, 76–7
Industrial Conciliation Act (1924), 74
influenza epidemic (1918), 43
influx control, 43–4, 73–4, 61, 98, 108–9, 123–4, 126; see also pass laws
Inkatha Freedom Party, 138, 139–40, 141, 143, 144, 145
Inkatha ka Zulu: foundation (1922–3), 82; refounded (1975), 118; in 1980s–1990s, 127, 133–4; conflict with ANC, 139; see also Inkatha Freedom Party
Iron age settlement, 6–7
Israelites, 54
Izwi Labantu, 80

Jabavu, John, 80, 85
Jameson raid (1895), 28
Johannesburg, 29, 41; housing in, 42, 61; see also Alexandra, Doornfontein, gold mining, Newclare, Orlando, Rand Revolt, Sophiatown, Soweto

Kadalie, Clements, 53
Kempton Park negotiations (1993), 140–2
Kgosana, Philip, 107
Khayelitsha, 126
Khoikhoi, 6, 9–10, 35, 66–7
kholwa farmers, 36, 46, 82

Kimberley: 'Black Flag' revolt, 38;
housing in, 42; *see also*
diamond mining
Kliptown, 105
Kruger, Paul, 24; and South
African War, 28
KwaMashu, 134
KwaNdebele, 135

Labour Party, *see* South African
Labour Party
Land Act, *see* Natives Land Act
Langa, 61; 1960 march from, 107;
Poqo in, 115
Langalibalele, 22
Leballo, Potlako, 106
Lebowa, 135
Lembede, Anton, 86, 106
Lesotho, 24, 25, 32; and migrant
labour, 44–5; and PAC, 115;
and peasant farming, 46;
South African attack on, 125
liberalism, Cape, 68–9
Liberal Party, 79, 104, 106
Lutuli, Albert, 100, 104, 106

Macmillan, Harold, 107
Malan, D. F., 90
Malan, Magnus, 125, 131
Mandela, Nelson, 86, 114, 137,
141, 143, 144, 145
Mangope, Lucas, 143
Manifesto of the Azanian People
(1983), 128
Marabastad, 62
marabi, 62–3
Marketing Act (1937), 58
Mass Democratic Movement
(MDM), 136–7
Master and Servant Amendment
Act (1926), 60
Masters and Servants Ordinance
(1841), 68
Matanzima, Kaiser, 113
Mbeki, Thabo, 144

Mfecane, 13–14
Mfengu, 46
Mgijima, Enoch, 55
migrant labour, pre-industrial, 17,
36–7; and mining industry, 27,
39, 44–6
Milner, Alfred, 28; and
Reconstruction administration,
32
Mines and Works Act (1911), 41,
81
Mines and Works Amendment Act
(1926), 74
mining industry, *see* diamond
mining, gold mining
Moshoeshoe, 16
Mozambique, 6, 20, 27, 115, 119,
122, 125, 126
Msimang, Selby, 53
Mxenge, Victoria, 134

Namibia, 32, 90, 98, 122, 125, 138
Nasionale Pers, 89
Natal, foundation of colony, 15;
and Zululand, 22–3; land
control in, 35–6, 46, 48;
franchise in, 70, 71; *see also*
Shepstone system
Natal Native Congress, 80
National Committee of Liberation,
114
National Education Crisis
Committee, 131
National Forum, 128
National Liberation League, 85
National Party: under Hertzog, 75,
87, 90; Gesuiwerde (later
Herenigde) Nasionale Party,
87, 90, 91–2; in power (from
1948), 98–9, 108; changing
support base (1980s), 122,
136, 138; in 1994 election,
143–4
National Security Management
System, 131

167

National Union of South African Students (NUSAS), 116, 128
Native Administration Act (1927), 74, 78–9
Native Affairs Act (1920), 74–5
Native Affairs Commission (1932), 59
Native Affairs Department, 59, 74, 78, 96, 98, 102; see also Bantu Affairs Department
Native Bills (1927), 75, 77
Native Educational Association, 80
Native Laws Amendment Act (1937), 61
Native Trust and Land Act (1936), 60
Natives (Urban Areas) Act (1923), 43, 62
Natives (Urban Areas) Amendment Act (1955), 98, 108
Natives Land Act (1913), 49–50, 76, 81; repealed, 137, 145
Natives Representative Council, 96
Natives Resettlement Act (1954), 96
Ndebele, 13, 24
necklacing, 131
Newclare, 44
Nicholls, Heaton, 77
Nkomati Accord (1984), 125–6
Non-European Unity Movement (NEUM), 85, 104, 115; and Black Consciousness, 117, 128
Note, Jan, 41

Orange Free State: foundation of, 16; land control in, 47, 48; franchise, 70
Ordinance 49 (1828), 68
Ordinance 50 (1828), 68
Orlando, 62, 64; ANC branch in, 106
Ossewa Brandwag, 92

Paarl, Poqo uprising in (1962), 115

Pact government, 53, 58, 60, 74
Pan Africanist Congress (PAC): foundation, 106; campaigns (1959–60), 107; banned (1960), 107, 108; after banning, 114–6; and Black Consciousness, 116–17; unbanning, 137; in 1994 election, 143, 144
pass laws, 61, 67, 73–4, 98, 122–3; campaigns against, 51–2, 73, 100–1, 107; abolition of, 123–4, 126
Patriots (1780s), 10
peasant farming, 46–7
Pedi, 15, 17, 21–2; and South African War, 29; and migrant labour, 44
Pietermaritzburg: segregation in, 42–3; UDF and Inkatha conflict in, 133–4
Pim, Howard, 77, 78
Plaatje, Sol, 50, 80, 82, 83
Pondoland, 24, 47, 69, 102, 103
poor whites, 48, 59
Population Registration Act (1950), 95–6; repealed, 137
Poqo, 114–15
Port Elizabeth, 11, 35, 61; strikes, 53; segregation in, 42; and Defiance Campaign, 100
Pretoria, 29, 32; segregation in, 96; Umkhonto attack (1985), 131; see also Marabastad
Programme of Action (1949), 87, 100
Progressive Federal Party (PFP), 133
Promotion of Bantu Self-Governing Act (1959), 110

Queenstown, 46

Rand Revolt (1922), 52
Reddingsdaadfons, 91

168

Representation of Natives Act
(1936), 75
Republic, declaration of (1961),
107
Reservation of Separate Amenities
Act (1953), 96
Retief, Piet, 12
Rhodes, Cecil: and South African
War, 26, 28; and mining
industry, 38
Rhodesia, see Zimbabwe
Riekert Commission (1979), 123
rinderpest epidemic (1896–7), 25,
46
Robben Island, 115
Rolong Tswana, 16, 24
Rubicon address (1985), 135
Rubusana, Walter, 80

San, 6, 7, 9–10, 35
sanctions, economic, 86, 135
Sand River Convention (1852), 16
Sanlam, 89, 91
Santam, 89
Sauer report (1946), 92, 93
School Board Act (1905), 69
segregation: roots of, 66–72; system
of, 72–9; reform and removal
of, 124, 136
Sekhukhune, 22, 29
Sekhukhuneland, 102, 135
Seme, Pixley, 83, 85
Separate Development, 109–110,
111–13
Sesotho Tsala ea Batho, 80
Shaka, 14
sharecropping, 47, 49
Sharpeville shootings (1960), 107;
Sharpeville Day, 129
shebeens, 62, 101
Shepstone, Theophilus, 20, 22, 71
Shepstone system, 71–2, 75
Simonstown, 19, 99
Sisulu, Walter, 86, 114

slavery: at the Cape, 8, 11, 34–5,
66–7, 68; as cause of
Mfecane, 14
Slums Act (1934), 62
Smuts, Jan, 32; and Rand Revolt,
42; and segregation, 78; and
World War II, 91; and 1948
election, 93–4
Sobukwe, Robert, 106
Social Darwinism, 65
Sofasonke movement, 64
Soga, Allan, 80
Sophiatown, 42, 44, 62, 96, 100,
103
Sotho, 13, 16, 24; labour in the
Cape, 37
South African Agricultural Union,
109
South African Coloured People's
Organisation, 105
South African Communist Party
(SACP), see Communist Party
of South Africa
South African Labour Party, 51,
53, 74, 91, 92
South African Native Affairs
Commission (SANAC), 73,
75–6
South African Native Congress, 80,
81
South African Native National
Congress, see African National
Congress
South African Republic, see
Transvaal
South African Students'
Organisation, 116
South African War (1899–1902),
25–31, 89
South West Africa, see Namibia
South West African People's
Organisation (SWAPO), 122,
125, 138
Soutpansberg, 15, 102

169

Soweto: establishment of, 96; uprising (1976), 119–20
Spanish flu (1918), *see* influenza epidemic
Stallard Commission, 43–4
Standard Bank, 88
State Security Council, 125, 131
Status Quo Act (1918), 51, 52
Stellenbosch University, 89
Stock Exchange, closure (1985), 135
strikes: of dockworkers (1919), 53; of farmworkers in western Cape (late 1920s), 57, 84; of mineworkers (1907–22), 51–2, (1940s), 64, 102; of Johannesburg municipal workers (1918), 51, 82; Indian strike (1913), 85; African strikes made illegal (1953), 97; in early 1970s, 118; Cape Town meat workers (1980), 127
Stubbs, Ernest, 77
Suppression of Communism Act (1950), 97
Swazi, 13, 15
Swaziland, 24, 32, 115, 125

Tambo, Oliver, 86
Tanzania, 115
Ten Point Programme (1943), 85
Terreblanche, Eugene, 141
Thatcher, Margaret, 135, 136
Thlaping Tswana, 21, 45
Tomlinson Commission (1955), 110
Torch Commando, 97
total strategy, 122–6
trade unions: recognition of, 51, 52, 74; African unions, 53, 64, 97, 123, 127; in Cape Town, 69, 84; Afrikaner unions, 91; growth in 1980s, 127; *see also* Council for Non-European

Trade Unions, Industrial and Commercial Workers' Union
Transitional Executive Council (1993–4), 141
Transkei: conquest of, 24; farming and land tenure in, 46, 59, 69; rural protest movements, 54; Bantustan, 111, 112; Poqo in, 115
Transkei Constitution Act (1963), 111
Transvaal: foundation of republic, 16; franchise in, 70; British annexation (1877–81) 22, 24, 89; expansion of, 24; and South African War, 26–7; land control in, 36, 47
Transvaal Native Congress, 51–2
Treason Trial, 105, 108
Tregardt, Louis, 12
trekboers, expansion at the Cape, 8–9, 11–12; in Natal, 15; in Transvaal and highveld, 16; *see also* Great Trek
Treurnicht, Andries, 122
tricameral constitution (1983), 124, 127–8
Tsonga, 15; and migrant labour, 45
Tswana, 17; and South African War, 29–30; and migrant labour, 45; *see also* Rolong, Thlaping
Tutu, Desmond, 136

Uitenhage shootings (1985), 129
Umkhonto we Sizwe, 114, 131, 141, 145
Umlazi, 134
Union, formation of, 32
United Democratic Front (UDF), 128–9, 130, 133–4, 135; banned, 131
United Nations, 86, 107
United Party, 75, 92, 98, 99

United Workers Union of South
Africa (UWUSA), 127, 133
Unity movement, see Non-European
Unity Movement
University Christian Movement,
116
Urban Foundation, 125

Vaal triangle uprising (1984), 129,
130
vagrancy proposals in the Cape, 68
Venda, 15, 24; Bantustan, 111
Vereeniging, Treaty of, 29, 31
Verwoerd, Hendrik, 96, 99, 107,
109, 110
Viljoen, Constand, 142
Vorster, John, 122

Wellington movement, 55
WHAM policy, 125
Wiehahn Report (1979), 123, 127
Witdoeke, 131

Witzieshoek, 102

Xhosa: conflicts with settlers
10–11, 17–18; cattle killing,
17–18; labour in the Cape, 37
Xuma, Alfred, 85

Youth League, 86–7

Zambia, 115, 136
Zeerust, 102
Zimbabwe, 6, 7, 26, 32, 115, 122,
125, 136, 138
Zulu: and Mfecane, 13–14, 15;
conquest of, 22–3; and South
African War, 29; and migrant
labour, 45–6; chief's powers
bolstered, 76–7; see also
ethnicity, Inkatha
Zululand, 23; Bantustan, 112, 135
Zwelithini, King Goodwill, 143,
145